# 25 SOLUTION
## YOUR IDENTITY IN CHRIST

# STOP Letting the World
# Be the BOSS of
# YOU!

# Jenn Chloupek, M.Ed. and
# Lauren E. Miller, M.Ed.

EDGE G⊕D IN PRESS

Published by Edge God In Press
www.EdgeGodIn.com

For permission contact Lauren at info@LaurenEMiller.com

Scripture taken from the HOLY BIBLE, TODAY'S NEW INTERNATIONAL VERSION®. TNIV®. Copyright © 2001, 2005 by International Bible Society. Used by permission of Zondervan. All rights reserved worldwide.

Cover design & Book format by DocUmeant Designs
www.DocUmeantDesigns.com

Published in the United States of America

For inquiries about volume orders, please contact:
Lauren E Miller at info@LaurenEMiller.com

ISBN: 9780999417225 15.95

# DEDICATION

We dedicate this book to Jesus Christ of Nazareth, who was not confined by status or the opinions of other people. In profound surrender to God's will and humility, Jesus gave up His own life on earth to save ours . . .

## One Solitary Life

He was born in an obscure village
The child of a peasant woman
He grew up in another obscure village
Where he worked in a carpenter shop
Until he was thirty

He never wrote a book
He never held an office
He never went to college
He never visited a big city

He never travelled more than two hundred miles
From the place where he was born
He did none of the things
Usually associated with greatness
He had no credentials but himself
He was only thirty-three

His friends ran away
One of them denied him
He was turned over to his enemies
And went through the mockery of a trial
He was nailed to a cross between two thieves
While dying, his executioners gambled for his clothing
The only property he had on earth

When he was dead
He was laid in a borrowed grave
Through the pity of a friend

Nineteen centuries have come and gone
And today Jesus is the central figure of the human race
And the leader of mankind's progress
All the armies that have ever marched
All the navies that have ever sailed
All the parliaments that have ever sat
All the kings that ever reigned put together
Have not affected the life of mankind on earth
As powerfully as that one solitary life

Dr James Allan © 1926

# CONTENTS

Dedication . . . . . . . . . . . . . . . . . . . . . . . . . . . . . . . . . . . . . . . . . iii

Foreword . . . . . . . . . . . . . . . . . . . . . . . . . . . . . . . . . . . . . . . . vii

Introduction . . . . . . . . . . . . . . . . . . . . . . . . . . . . . . . . . . . . xxi

What Determines the Direction of Your Heart? . . . . . . . . . . . 1

Hello My Name Is . . . . . . . . . . . . . . . . . . . . . . . . . . . . . . . . . . . 5

Stand Up for Your Identity . . . . . . . . . . . . . . . . . . . . . . . . . . 10

Flip Self-Focus to Other-Focused & Joy Returns . . . . . . . . . . 14

"If" Statements that Rob . . . . . . . . . . . . . . . . . . . . . . . . . . . . 18

Misplaced Identity: You are Not Who You Were . . . . . . . . . . 22

Greed Breeds Anxiety & Shrinks Confidence . . . . . . . . . . . . 26

A Key to Freedom You Want to Know . . . . . . . . . . . . . . . . . 32

Mugged by the Mirror . . . . . . . . . . . . . . . . . . . . . . . . . . . . . 36

Who is the Real You? . . . . . . . . . . . . . . . . . . . . . . . . . . . . . . . 40

How to Recognize Pride vs. a Prideful Nature . . . . . . . . . . . 44

Three Identity Busters . . . . . . . . . . . . . . . . . . . . . . . . . . . . . . 48

Polluted Position . . . . . . . . . . . . . . . . . . . . . . . . . . . . . . . . . . 52

Aroma: What is Your Scent? . . . . . . . . . . . . . . . . . . . . . . . . . 56

Flip Rejection into Direction . . . . . . . . . . . . . . . . . . . . . . . . 60

Live W.O.W. . . . . . . . . . . . . . . . . . . . . . . . . . . . . . . . . . . . . . 65

Re-boot Your Identity with One Question . . . . . . . . . . . . . . 72

Abracadabra! . . . . . . . . . . . . . . . . . . . . . . . . . . . . . . . . . . . . . 78

You Know What You Need to Know . . . . . . . . . . . . . . . . . . 84

Fallen, Not Forgotten . . . . . . . . . . . . . . . . . . . . . . . . . . . . . . 91

A Three Step Prison Break . . . . . . . . . . . . . . . . . . . . . . . . . . 97

Six Logical Levels for Transformation . . . . . . . . . . . . . . . . . 109

God Can Move Mountains . . . . . . . . . . . . . . . . . . . . . . . . . . . . . 119

Holding Pattern . . . . . . . . . . . . . . . . . . . . . . . . . . . . . . . . . . . . 124

Two Identity Thieves: Your To-Do List & The Drug
    of Approval . . . . . . . . . . . . . . . . . . . . . . . . . . . . . . . . . . . 132

Conclusion & Support Materials . . . . . . . . . . . . . . . . . . . . . . . 141

About the Authors . . . . . . . . . . . . . . . . . . . . . . . . . . . . . . . . . . 147

Additional Support Resources . . . . . . . . . . . . . . . . . . . . . . . . . 149

# FOREWORD
*Jenn Chloupek / Lauren E Miller*

Our forward includes our own personal identity theft stories. Perhaps you will mix some elements from your own journey into our stories of identity theft. The main point here is to know that you are not alone. Four basic needs tie us all together in the human experience: the need for safety and connection and the need for meaning and significance.

Too often we find ourselves rummaging around in the world looking to meet those four basic needs with "trinkets" that never fully satisfy. They consistently leave us empty handed and longing for more.

For more of what? For more of what our Savior, Jesus Christ, died to give us and the world can never offer.

Identity theft occurs when our sense of worth and value is linked to the outside world, rising and falling depending on how the world judges us at that moment in time.

Identity theft is an exhausting vicious cycle that bobbles us around like a cat toy, clawed by the next "shiny" object that captures our attention. It breeds insecurity, embarrassment, fear, doubt, and too often panic and despair.

Had enough? DIA! (Hebrew for ENOUGH) Enough of feeling less than, not enough, insecure, overwhelmed! The devil comes to kill and destroy (rob your sense of security, connection, significance and meaning, tricking you to believe that you need something outside of you to know you have worth and value).

> *"Jesus has come into the world that we may have life and have it to the fullest"* (John 10:10).

Similar to a hamster running on a hamster wheel, no matter how fast you run to keep up with what the world says you need to be, look like, say, and do in order to have worth and value, it's time.

Time to come home and rest in the presence of the One who calls you by name and says: "I SEE YOU . . . YOU MATTER."

This book includes pathways, tools, and techniques designed to:
- Empower you with the ability to take back your identity and return it to its rightful owner: God.
- Remind you that you matter. The lover of your soul is the hound from heaven and will continue to bring you back to what you truly long for: a personal relationship with God through Jesus Christ of Nazareth who died to win you back from the worldly game of life.

*"It is for freedom that Christ has set us free. Stand firm then, and do not let yourselves be burdened again by a yoke of slavery* [to the shiny objects of the world that leave you longing for more of what can never truly satisfy]" (Galatians 5:1).

Join us as we pull back the curtain and let you, the reader, observe our identity hijack "earth school" experiences that caused us to forget *whose* we are on this journey of life.

## Jenn's Identity Theft & Restoration Story

### GOD, SIN, CHRIST, YOU

**God** created the world which was good and beautiful.

**Sin** entered the world through Adam and Eve.

**Christ** is the greatest love story ever told to redeem mankind and restore our relationship with God our Father. Christ died for our sins so that those who believe may spend eternity in Heaven with God our Father.

**You** have a choice and decision to make for eternity.

I can vividly remember as a small child giving my life to Christ during Sunday school class. I must have been in first grade. I remember the Sunday school teacher explaining that there was a God who created the Universe and that He loved us very much and desired a relationship with us however sin separated us from God.

She then began to share the Good News that God sent His son Jesus to die on the cross for our sins and that we had a choice to receive Christ as our Savior and to have our sin blotted out so that we could be white as snow standing before God.

I knew without a doubt at that young age that God planted eternity in my heart. And I prayed for Jesus to wash away my sins that personally nailed Him to the cross to make me white as snow.

One of my life verses comes from Philippians 1, *"being confident of this, that he who began a good work in you will carry it on to completion until the day of Christ Jesus"* (V. 6).

I am fully confident that at the young age of six God began a good work in me when I said that prayer inviting Jesus into my heart to be Lord and Savior of my life. I surrendered fully as much as I knew how to at the tender age of six.

God has always been with me ever since that day, even when I might have moved and distanced myself through the years, God remained constant. I moved, he did not.

For the most part, life was smooth sailing during my elementary school years. I was an only child from a middle-class family. We attended Sunday school and church on a regular basis.

I found my middle school years trying. I was unsure of my identity and found myself "proving my worth" to feel loved, accepted, valued, etc. I farmed out my identity mostly to other people, positions, popularity, and possessions. I had a momentary lapse and forgot who was sitting on the throne of my life. I yearned to fit in and did just about anything to do so.

High school years weren't much better. I was pretty much friends with all the friend groups which had me searching for my identity in others. I knew that God had placed eternity in my heart and that He had His hand on me, however I was trying to fill that God-shaped space with everything but God.

> *"He has made everything beautiful in its time. He has also set eternity in the human heart; yet no one can fathom what God has done from beginning to end"* (Ecclesiastes 3:11).

God put eternity into the heart of man so that in our longing and confusion we will seek Him, and that is exactly what God did with me to call me back to Him.

I felt this unexplainable pull that led me to a group called Young Life. I was searching for my original identity that was hijacked by the world.

I longed to renew my true identity in Christ. I wanted to know that I was enough and that I didn't have to prove my worth in destructive ways.

I remember having a Young Life group at my house. I felt God during this period of my life. During a Young Life camp in high school at Saranac Lake in New York, I re-dedicated my life to Christ.

When I sat alone in silence for a long time, I knew that this re-dedication would not be easy. God and the Holy Spirit were asking me to give up some major aspects of my life in order to be a true follower of Christ.

I often go back to my life verse from Philippians 1:6, *"being confident of this, that he who began a good work in you will carry it on to completion until the day of Christ Jesus."*

God allows the confusion, the challenging questions, the yearning desires, all of it, so that we will earnestly pursue Him.

Again, God began a good work in me at age six and He was slowly teaching me what sanctification means.

I would say that my adult life until I was 40 was one foot in the world and one foot out of the world. I continued to struggle with where to place my identity which turned into years of Godly lessons in what not to do.

I was married at 20 thinking it would last a lifetime yet found myself divorced at 33. The divorce was a direct result of me still trying to pursue my identity in the shiny entrapments of my finite world. I was blinded by what the world had to offer and pursued activities that drained me leaving me longing for satisfaction.

I had strayed away from the Lord and tried to find my identity in the world. I stepped outside of God's umbrella of protection, and praise God, He called me back as I still had ears to listen and a heart that was convicted. Just like the shepherd that Jesus is, he left the 99 sheep to come and get me!

> *"What do you think? If a man owns a hundred sheep, and one of them wanders away, will he not leave the ninety-nine on the hills and go to look for the one that wandered off?"* (Matthew 18:12).

Divorce was a label that shaped my identity. I was a divorced mom with two boys. It was a label that I never wanted to wear to shape my identity, however I had lived a life that resulted in divorce. I was living a double life while lying to myself and to God.

Wearing a couple of identity masks can be exhausting! I needed to plug in to the greatest source of refreshment . . . Jesus Christ.

Trying to maintain different images, appearances, and identities mired in the lie of freedom was a snare Satan used to keep me stuck in a pattern that was not working for me, or for the Kingdom of God.

The lies the enemy whispered sounded good. I heard, "you deserve this, this won't hurt, this is innocent, . . .". All of this left me wanting more and being ashamed of who I was becoming.

During this time, I lived my life in and out of church.

One day I decided enough is enough. I was exhausted and was also recently diagnosed with Meniere's Disease that can be debilitating at times and yet it was a gift in that the experience led me to surrender before God.

This grand disease left me in the hospital and took me months to get back to a somewhat normal state. I eventually lost most of the hearing in my right ear. A new identity: deaf in one ear.

At this point in my life, I threw up my hands in true surrender. I knew my health was being compromised as a result of my choices. Usually Meniere's Disease flares up when the body gives up due to stress.

The stress of living multiple identities had taken a toll on my body and I was done. I had come to the end of myself and finally gave God control over my life.

Living life trying to prove my worth to anyone other than God is still a constant battle for me. Now I have the awareness when this happens, and I have a choice now to respond differently.

Talk about true freedom!

Free to be me. In this life I have compared myself with others, strived to be someone I wasn't created to be and have allowed others to define me.

My biggest renewal in identity came when God revealed that I can experience true freedom in Christ, which resulted in a freedom to be me.

This freedom to be myself in Christ has *no price*. Jesus has paid the *ultimate price* on the cross for me.

> *"I am the good shepherd. The good shepherd lays down his life for the sheep"* (John 10:11).

Jesus is the good shepherd and has laid down His life to save our lives!

Pause and reflect on this truth: Jesus is the good shepherd and has laid down His life to save our lives!

Would anyone else do this for you?

Next time I try to farm out my identity to someone else or something else, I want to remember what the Good Shepherd has done for me.

My story is that of the wandering sheep. There have been many times that I have remained in the fold, however, there have been times that I have stepped out over the last 40 years of my life.

God has been faithful with the work he started in my life at the tender age of six.

Each time I strayed, the Good Shepherd came and found me and brought me back into the fold, and I am forever grateful.

*"Suppose one of you has a hundred sheep and loses one of them. Doesn't he leave the ninety-nine in the open country and go after the lost sheep until he finds it?"* (Luke 15:4).

## Lauren's Identity Theft & Restoration Story

Stress is the power you give to outside circumstance to define your worth, value, and capability. Don't let the outer voices and experiences in the world write the script in your mind.

It is for FREEDOM that Christ has set you free, stand firm and don't allow yourself to be burdened by the yoke of slavery to the opinions and reactions of people around you (Galatians 5:1). Jesus was not concerned with status or the opinions of other people . . . why are we?

I refer to the majority of my teenage years as my "B.C." days: before Jesus Christ won me over and set me free from the prison created by the drug of approval and attachment to shiny objects that robbed my inner peace, confidence, and joy.

Yup, I was completely submerged in the "Drug of Approval" and "Attachment to Shiny Objects".

**DRUG OF APPROVAL:** needing other people around me to tell me and show me that I had worth and value. One of the biggest negative side effects of this drug caused me to rise and fall depending upon how the world judged me at each moment. Basically, this drug says: "I need you to tell me that I am okay all the time."

**ATTACHMENT TO SHINY OBJECTS:** Anything outside of me that sparkled and caught my attention along with my sense of worth and value. Before I knew it, I spilled out of myself. I was Gollum from *The Lord of the Rings* in the cave clinging to my "Precious Ring" thinking I needed "it" whatever "it" was to feel that I was accepted, valued, included and enough. Negative side-effects: A vicious cycle of discontentment and not-enough-ness, sleepless nights filled with endless worry around two needy, insecure questions: the need to know why things happen as they do AND the need to know how things will turn out. An attachment is an emotional state of clinging due to the belief that you cannot be happy, secure, and content without your "shiny objects." It's smoke and mirrors and trickery that left me empty-handed, discontent, and craving more.

The main serpents that would crash my happy party included: envy, insecurity, jealousy, negative rumination (thinking a thought over and over and over again), and comparison.

The behavior that spilled out of me as a result of the Drug of Approval and Attachment to Shiny Objects included:

- **LYING:** Fueled by the fear of disapproval or not getting to do what I wanted to do.
- **UGLY TALK:** Cursing when things didn't go my way. I remember when I was 16 a dear friend confronted me about the foul language that came out of my mouth. He said it wasn't very attractive to which I responded: "What the "F" are you talking about? My "B.C." days at their best.
- **MANIPULATION:** Fueled by not feeling like I was enough.
- **DRINKING/SMOKING:** Even though I didn't like it, I wanted to fit in.

I was in a total identity crisis.

I didn't know *whose* I was, why I was here or why it really mattered. I was searching for the living among the dead. (Luke 24:5) I looked to the world (people, circumstances, outcomes) to give me what only God can give me: a sense of safety and connection, meaning and significance. It was like trying to squeeze lemon juice from a banana . . . no matter how hard I squeeze I will never get lemon juice.

When I think about it, it's a pretty cool alarm system God wired into our "earth suit".

Every time I venture outside my *interior castle* (my inner world with God as St. Teresa of Avila refers to it) and look for my identity outside in the world I am left empty handed . . . oh, I might get a momentary hit of pleasure yet it is quickly swallowed up by an intense longing for more.

Jesus asked the disciples in John 6, after some had walked away due to a lack of understanding: are you going to leave? To which Peter responded, *"Lord, where else do we go? You have the words of eternal life . . . You are the Holy One of God."*

Basically, Peter was saying Jesus, You have everything I need for true life, godliness, peace, joy and everlasting life . . . are you kidding? I'm going wherever You go, with You I lack nothing.

St. Augustine said that victory lies in our ability to give our spirit permission to guide our flesh verses our giving our flesh permission to guide our spirit.

Well, I can tell you this, before Jesus Christ of Nazareth made His way to the throne of my heart, my flesh was guiding my spirit and dragging my identity through the muck of the worldly trappings along with it.

The summer of 1984 my parents took me and my two brothers and sister to a Christian ranch in Colorado for a family vacation, my mom picked up on the fact that I was losing myself in the world, just sayin' . . . of course they didn't tell me it was a Christian ranch in case you are wondering, I figured it out on my own when I was invited to a Bible Study group one evening.

Now, because I had mastered the art of fitting into any group, I actually pretended to be a Christian, how hard can that be right?

I zipped up the best version of me that evening. Everyone seemed to buy what I was selling (there is that manipulation behavior crashing the scene) until I was asked to read from the book of Psalms which I pronounced Palms and then began flipping through the New Testament looking for it . . . not that you have to know where the books of the Bible are to be a Christian, until a kind Christian who was sitting next to me on the couch helped me out.

I remember sitting back and listening to the readings from the book of John and feeling this longing for what was being said . . . I was instantly curious and wanted to hear more.

The conversations that evening were so different than I had ever been a part of with my peer group . . . I was literally blown away by the depth of conviction, confidence, sense of purpose, and identity that surrounded me in that room. I went along with the prayers and felt this presence I didn't understand yet I knew I wanted more of.

Now, I think it's important for you to know that I had another ulterior motive attending that Bible Study that evening . . . I had a secret crush on one of the wranglers at the ranch and heard he would be attending.

I remember watching him pray before he ate his food and I was so moved by it. God is the best multi-level marketer I know and He uses ALL of the available resources to win over the hearts of His children, I was no exception.

Regardless, when I walked away that evening, I didn't know it at the time, but I was walking away from my former way of living life . . . I would never be the same again. You can say Jesus had me at hello.

When I snuck back into my cabin, I distinctly remember hitting my knees and praying something like: *"Lord, I want what they have. I want a relationship with You like they have; I want to know You and what it's like to feel your love for me. Come into my life and change me from the inside out."*

Instantly I felt a profound presence and I slept deeper and more peacefully than I had slept in a long time.

When we got back from our family trip I couldn't stop thinking of Jesus.

One night I went into my parent's room and asked my mom if she had a bible I could read. It's funny looking back now because my mom was trying to keep her cool and act really casual yet inside, she was freaking out that her wild and crazy daughter was asking for a bible.

Can you imagine? My mom knew what I was doing most of the time, she actually wept in front of me about a year before we went on our family vacation to the ranch, begging me not to lie anymore and that she didn't know what to do . . . it breaks my heart thinking about how my behavior caused her so many sleepless nights and there I stood before her asking if she had a Holy Bible I could read? Who does that? Someone who had a personal encounter with the lover of her soul.

Jesus' healing and restoration is not confined by time or intensity. An example of this comes from John 8:10 when Jesus encounters a woman caught in adultery and He says to her: Is there anyone here to condemn you? She replied through her tears, "No one sir." Then Jesus said, "then go and sin no more."

That was it, one personal encounter with Christ led to repentance which ignited and put into motion instantaneously a resurrected life.

I call it the ERR effect: "Encounter" the love and forgiveness of Jesus. "Repent", not out of guilt but out of love for Jesus. The Holy Spirit moved me into behavior that reflected Jesus presence in my life, I stopped saying the "F" bomb instantly, didn't even try, it just happened, other behavior took more time yet my heart was changed forever.

Pick up your mat and go, get up and step into the "Resurrected" life Jesus died to give you.

I fell in love with a Christian man soon after I invited Jesus to sit on the throne of my identity to remind me of "whose" I was and all of the amazing perks that go along with that relationship on a daily basis. One year after I fell in love, he was killed in a car accident. God used him to help anchor my faith early on.

At the end of my senior year in High School after his death I remember crying out to God and hearing back a whisper that invited me closer: *Make your faith your own.*

I had attached some of my sense of security in my faith to the relationship I had with my boyfriend and Jesus gently reminded me that in Him, I lack nothing.

I grieved well into my first year of college and beyond; yet in the midst of the grief I had a profound sense of comfort and connection to Jesus, he knew the depth of my pain and carried me through it all.

I entered into ministry via FCA in college and then youth and adult ministries post-graduation. Jesus saved me from the Drug of Approval and Attachment to Shiny Objects and called me to pass it along.

Flash forward another 20 years, a marriage and three beautiful children later, I found myself knocked to the floor . . . literally, after a phone call that began with: "Are you sitting down." The doctor on the other line proceeded to tell me that the results from the biopsy revealed that I had a very aggressive form of breast cancer.

Jesus entered the eye of the storm with me, just as he did when I was 16 and tossed about like a cat toy by worldly attachments. I knew I was not alone and that made all the difference in the outcomes I experienced.

It was the perfect storm, yet I learned that God does His greatest work in the darkest nights. With every storm, Jesus comes too.

I was diagnosed with cancer one week prior to my final divorce court date. I was the only one in my family to get divorced, I believe in marriage with all my heart yet mine did not work out. Thankfully God has blessed me with a second chance, I have been happily remarried for ten years.

In less than a two-year period of time I went through a divorce, a double mastectomy, 16 chemotherapy treatments, six weeks of daily radiation, 14 surgeries due to $3^{rd}$ degree burns on my chest from the radiation/chemo combination they graphed my back onto my front . . . so now I really don't know if I'm coming or going most days, I also had a MRSA staph infection due to an open wound on my chest that I had for a year (makes me wonder how many people walk around with "unseen" wounds . . . let me assure you, God sees, cares, and restores).

I never knew how attached I was to my hair, breasts or image in the mirror until they were all gone.

After taking my three children with my mom to give my hair away to Locks of Love I came home and snuck away in my room to pray for strength. I remember I was weeping deeply over the loss of my hair and image along with fear when I was interrupted by two little hands placed on my head.

My 10-year-old son had snuck up behind me and said, "Mommy, don't cry your soul still has hair." Obviously, he had been prompted by the Holy Spirit to say those words because instantly the tears dried up and I remembered "whose" I was and what I wasn't.

The devil prowled around night after night trying to get me to buy into the lies that fueled fear, doubt, and worry. He was enticing me to give more authority to the diagnosis than to the strength of God within me to overcome. Again, and again I would resist the attacks in the name of Jesus Christ of Nazareth and choose life and restoration in Christ. The doctors were trying to get me five more years of life, that was 13 years ago.

> *"Be of sober spirit, be on the alert. Your adversary, the devil prowls around like a roaring lion seeking someone to devour. But resist him, firm in your faith, knowing that the same experiences of suffering are being accomplished by your brethren who are in the world. After you have suffered for a little while, the God of all grace, who called you to His eternal glory in Christ, will Himself perfect, confirm, strengthen and establish you. To Him be dominion forever and ever. Amen"* (1 Peter 5:8-10).

I share my identity theft and restoration experience with you to let you know, reader, that you are not alone in your storm, transition or confusion. God is with you, whether you feel His presence or not he will never leave you or forsake you.

God adores you and has plans to prosper you and not to harm you, to remind your mind that you are His child, part of a royal priesthood, He delights in you and cares deeply about what breaks your heart or causes you to be confused. Ask, seek, and knock.

He is the hound from heaven and will chase you down to free you and restore your true identity in Him. All meaning and significance along with safety and connection flow from your relationship with the One who died to win you over from death to life.

One of the first verses I stored in my heart was Revelations 3:20, as it captures in a nutshell my identity theft and restoration story . . . Jesus knocked and knocked and knocked and knocked . . . when I stepped away from the screams of the world enough to hear His gentle, kind whisper . . . I remembered whose I was and I have never been the same since.

> *"Behold, I stand at the door, and knock: **if any man hears my voice, and open the door, I will come in to him, and will sup with him, and he with me.**"*

# INTRODUCTION
*STOP Letting the World Be the Boss of You!*
**25 Solutions to Refresh Your Identity in Christ**

**S**TOP: is a verb meaning to abandon a specific practice or habit, in this case, to abandon the habit of giving power to the world (people, circumstances, and experiences) to define your worth and value, sense of meaning, and significance. Stop letting the world be the boss of you! You didn't let your peers in preschool and kindergarten be the boss of you. When did you start giving your identity away to people, positions, and performance?

**SOLUTION:** A means of solving a problem.

**REFRESH:** VERB to give new strength or energy to; reinvigorate.

You refresh a URL to restore the connection to its original link resulting in a clear stronger connection.

When we refresh our identity in Christ, we restore our identity to its original link: to God. God is the lover of our souls through Jesus Christ in and through the power of the Holy Spirit that dwells within us.

**IDENTITY:** The fact of being who or what a person or thing is.

**JESUS CHRIST:** Lamb of God, Eternal Life, The First and the Last, The Alpha and Omega, the Word of God made flesh, only begotten Son of God, Savior of the world, Lion of Judah, Prince of Peace, the Lord of Glory, just to name a few.

As you read through this book you will notice we have offered you 25 areas to explore that give you, the reader, the opportunity to reinvigorate, re-establish, and refresh the life and strength to your identity in Christ, resulting in a transformation that will change your life for the better.

> As Paul says in Philippians 3, *"What is more, I consider everything a loss because of the surpassing worth of knowing Christ*

*Jesus my Lord, for whose sake I have lost all things. I consider them garbage, that I may gain Christ"* (V. 8).

What moved Paul to declare such a radical perspective of life?

Daily life on earth is filled with so many things, shiny objects and trinkets that captivate our time and attention.

What was it exactly that moved Paul to declare EVERYTHING a loss compared to the surpassing worth of knowing Christ Jesus as his Lord?

Perhaps it was the personal encounter he had on the road to Damascus that lead him to the end of himself and into the realization of his soul's knowing that when he came to the end of "self" and repented from behavior that compromised his relationship with God, it was then that he encountered the lover of his soul, his heart's longing was fulfilled in his encounter with Christ which resulted in a resurrected identity, purpose, and passion.

Paul experienced a radical identity resurrection.

How? He first had an encounter with the risen Lord on his way to bully believers in Christ.

Next, Paul fell on his face and declared in the midst of confession Jesus as Lord: "Who are You Lord?"

His identity went from being highly recognized among men to preaching and dying for the gospel message of Christ.

How is this possible?

Radical, unconditional love and identity restoration. The kind of love that makes absolutely no sense from an earthly perspective and results in a resurrected clarity around three questions:
- Who am I?
- Why am I here?
- What will it matter?

God's radical love for us poured out in the gift of His one and only Son. It is undeserved and yet freely given in spite of negative behavior to the one who asks, seeks, and opens the door of their heart: "Who are You Lord?"

*"Here I am! I stand at the door and knock. If anyone hears my voice and opens the door, I will come in and eat with them, and they with me"* (Revelation 3:20).

This book is all about remembering "whose" you are in Christ along with the ramifications surrounding that remembrance, your identity refreshment.

Identify theft is seen all throughout the Bible. Before we get into our **25 SOLUTIONS** for refreshing your identity in Christ, it is valuable to examine John the Baptist's public ministry.

John began his ministry before the first week of Jesus' ministry.

> *"Now this was John's testimony when the Jewish leaders in Jerusalem sent priests and Levites to ask him who he was. He did not fail to confess, but confessed freely, 'I am not the Messiah.'*
>
> *They asked him, 'Then who are you? Are you Elijah?'*
>
> *He said, 'I am not.'*
>
> *'Are you the Prophet?'*
>
> *He answered, 'No.'*
>
> *Finally, they said,' Who are you? Give us an answer to take back to those who sent us. What do you say about yourself?'*
>
> *John replied in the words of Isaiah the prophet, 'I am the voice of one calling in the wilderness," Make straight the way for the Lord.'"*
>
> *Now the Pharisees who had been sent questioned him, 'Why then do you baptize if you are not the Messiah, nor Elijah, nor the Prophet?'*
>
> *'I baptize with water,' John replied, 'but among you stands one you do not know. He is the one who comes after me, the thongs of whose sandals I am not worthy to untie.*
>
> *This all happened at Bethany on the other side of the Jordan, where John was baptizing"* (John 1:19–28).

John refused to compete with Jesus.

Instead of directing attention at himself, John points to Jesus and states that he is not even worthy to untie Jesus' sandals. John knows his position and identity in Christ.

However, fast forward a year. John's voice from prison sounded less certain, he was beginning to wonder if Jesus was truly the Messiah. *". . . Are you the one who was to come, or should we expect someone else?"* (Matthew 11:3). John's confidence in the Messiah is starting to decrease.

John has some doubt and is beginning to look through the lens of his own personal identity and expectations and not fully understanding that his expectations might be misaligned with Jesus' expectations.

John was still living in the flesh like we all are. His identity was being challenged by modern day worldly standards. God's Kingdom is not designed like our worldly kingdoms.

During our times of persecution, suffering, grief, loss, unmet longings, and addictions we too can wonder if Jesus is who we thought He was.

As a Christ-follower, self-concept is connected to the God-concept. If we begin to question who God is, then we begin to question our identity in Him. We are valuable because God is Creator. We are forgiven because God is Redeemer.

So, perhaps a question we might bump up against when we question our identity may be, "If God is not who we thought He was, then who are we?"

As you read through this book, you will meet on the pages, the Author of our faith, God. He is more than able to address the identity crisis His unexpected words and ways may trigger.

John was struggling with Jesus' actions. Somehow Jesus' actions were not aligning with John's expectations.

The gap between what Jesus was doing and what John thought Jesus should be doing was straining John's understanding of who Jesus was.

Some of the culprits of identity theft can seem unassu innocent to start. Some of the major identity theft offe our modern-day culture (power and possessions); succ marketplace (position); family and the way we were r the values that were passed down to us; relationships around us and the relationships we are involved in (popularity).

These culprits of identity theft don't seem very suspicious on paper, however at the very core, if left unchecked, they can rob us of our identity and tell us the lie that we don't belong here.

The first step as we navigate and unpack our identity journey is awareness.

The good news is you are in control of your thoughts, words, and actions_and when you become aware of a pick-pocketer of your identity, you are in control if you don't allow them to rob your identity and who you authentically are.

As I reflect on the previous year, and think about the moments and opportunities, I keep thinking back to one moment where someone's words had the potential to rob me of my identity: When that person told me that I was a great understudy, instead of focusing on all the good that the year was filled with, I was concerned with position.

Thankfully, I know my worth. I am now aware of and filter everything through the lens of coaching and questioning. I coach myself often and this was one of those moments.

When you find yourself in an identity theft moment, pause and ask yourself, what did I just give power away to? A conclusion? Assumption? Judgment? A lie that is not from God?

As you move forward in your life, try including a daily technique to help anchor your identity in Christ: start each day with an intentional declaration of who you are in Christ.

*I am:*
- Complete in Christ
- Worthy in Christ
- Loved and Adored by God

- Blessed by God
- Forgiven through Christ
- Strong in Christ
- Confident with Christ
- Competent in Christ
- Capable in Christ

Studies have revealed that to override negative self-talk you need to replace one negative thought with three positive thoughts to create a new messaging system in the brain.

The scripture backs this up: "*. . . take captive every thought to make it obedient to Christ*" (2 Corinthians 10:4-5).

And again, in Romans 12:2, "*Do not conform to the pattern of this world, but be transformed by the renewing of your mind.*"

Perhaps a remedy for identity theft lies in our ability to fast from negative thinking and linger in positive self-awareness: "*I am not the opinions of other people, an outcome or struggle . . . unless I choose to be.*"

*How is this possible you might say after a day of having your mind hijacked by negativity?*

> *Jesus looked at them and said, "With human beings this is impossible, but **with God all things are possible** [emphasis mine]*" (Matthew 19:26).

Throughout this book you will be asked to reflect on your life. Reflection leads to identification and action.

After each *Don't Let the World Be the Boss of You!* entry you will notice a section entitled: *Refresh Your Identity in Christ* which will offer you the opportunity to take action on the content learned. You will also be given an opportunity to write down the Ah-Ha moments you want to transfer into your life experience by using the L.O.V.E. learning acronym posted at the end of each entry.

We encourage you to spend some time after prayer to complete the L.O.V.E acronym to help you refresh your true identity in Christ!

Miller's L.O.V.E. Learning Circle™

L: **LEARN & LISTEN** *Ask the Holy Spirit: What's for me to refresh my identity in Christ?*

The process of learning is magnified when you tune into a specific personal value contained in the information you are exposed to.

As a second-degree black belt in TaeKwonDo I would mentally set my intention around the goals I wanted to achieve in the ring and for the most part my body would follow my focus. The same opportunity lies before you when it comes to learning and growth.

Mentally setting the stage for learning and growth increases the odds that you will in fact learn and grow.

The reticular activating system (RAS) located by the brain stem is a built-in system that is your closest friend or worst enemy simply because it will hunt and gather specific pieces of information that support your chosen view of reality.

As you step into each day of earth school, pray for the grace to listen closely in order to pick up on those pieces of information that align with the person you are committed to being in this world. Too often we give power to other people's opinions to define who we are and render ourselves vulnerable to false information and increased stress and anxiety.

We live in an information overload society and it's easy to get overwhelmed and paralyzed rather than empowered and motivated.

The next time you find yourself presented with new information, pause and ask yourself, "What's in it for me that will add meaning to my life and champion me into the best version of who I am in this world personally and professionally?"

Opinions, like clothing, can be put back on the rack. If it doesn't fit and it's not the right color release it and move on ASAP.

As you release pieces of information that do not add value to your current position in life, you clear out head trash and open up mental space to notice content that sparkles and supports your optimal learning and growth.

O: **OBSERVE**

Resurrect your childlike curiosity.

Jesus said that the Kingdom of God (the freedom, peace, confidence, and love that comes with it) belongs to the children. A practice of curiosity and fascination will catapult you into the space of absorbing content quickly.

When I facilitate a seminar or workshop, I invite participants to practice high noticing (intentional observation) around 1–3 specific gold nuggets of knowledge that are meant for them to find. How do you know when you find your knowledge nugget? It's when you perk up and understand the information you are receiving with interest. Similar to a treasure hunt, you seek out clues based on content that peaks your attention.

Engagement occurs when you identify with information you are exposed to that personally ignites the "Tell me more" button within. Just as Samuel from the Sacred Scriptures unlocked his ability to hear the voice of God by the simple statement: "Speak Lord, your servant is listening." Learning and listening walk through the archway of observation. Listening requires the commitment on your part to step away from your assumptions, judgments, and conclusions that hold you very small in life as they restrict your ability to see things from a bigger perspective of possibilities.

As a child, you simply existed in the present moment assimilating your observations, which gave you the ability to combine larger amounts of content quickly and create consistently.

As a child, you would capture with awe and wonder the small details of life that many adults overlook daily: a roly-poly butterfly or a snowflake. You were never left empty handed in your ability to create your reality.

## V: **VISUALIZE**

Our senses constantly process a blizzard of incoming externally generated information which we immediately and drastically triage, saving only the tiny fraction that seems most important for our purposes.

What causes some information to stick and other information to simply melt away?

Two elements are required for information to move past short-term memory into the vast storage center of long-term memory: a visual and a powerful emotion.

A visual can be created beyond the physical experience of sight. For example, you hear a song and smell a scent in the presence of a powerful positive emotional experience and the next time you hear that song or smell that scent you instantly pull up a visual that was created down to small details depending upon the strength of the emotional component (this can be of value to you or in some cases a painful memory).

Imagination and visualization walk hand and hand. As a child you constantly used the gift of your imagination to enrich your reality.

All things were possible for you because you believed they were: magical kingdoms, super hero powers and the ability to transform pillows and blankets into secret hideouts . . . members only. You would visualize what it would be like to have superpowers and believed you did which shifted your entire outlook. You did it back then and you can do it now.

The practical use of visualization in the learning environment looks like this: you learn something that peaks your attention because it relates to your personal or professional life experience so you pause and observe (you move closer to the content and perhaps engage in questions to learn more).

The next step to unlock learning and growth of valuable content is to visualize how this information will specifically shift your view of reality in a positive and meaningful way along with tuning into the emotional component of what you will look like, feel like, and sound like as you utilize the valuable content in daily life.

For example, you attend a seminar on How to Create & Sustain Meaningful Relationships. You learn about three reactive responses that block effective connection along with three responses that create instant connection and you write them down. You observe that you are highly engaged with the information and ask questions for clarity, because the content has value for you in your life personally and professionally. Visualize how you will identify and adjust specific behaviors, perceptions, and conclusions in order to effectively integrate new patterns of thought and behavior. When you visualize how the valuable content will impact your life for good you create an anchor for sustainable applicability.

As you read through the 25 solutions to refresh your identity in Christ, pause and visualize how you see the information shifting your behavior moving forward. Jesus consistently used visualization when he shared parables to anchor and put into motion new ways of thinking and acting (mustard seed, mountains, the prodigal son, the good Samaritan).

E: **EXPLORE**

Explore the specific forward action steps you will take to integrate the meaningful content you just learned into your daily life personally and professionally. This could include new content or fresh perspectives around old content. Basically, you learned something of value that has intrigued you, what do you want to do about it? Do you want to chalk it up as a fun learning experience and go back to life as you knew it or do you want to begin noticing and intentionally integrating the valuable content into your words, thoughts, deeds, and actions and expand the best version of you into your future?

When you explore with the intention of positive forward momentum you expand your influence factor. The first phase of emotional intelligence is to know what lights you up and what doesn't. Invite the Holy Spirit into each entry and ask what is for me Lord and what do you want me to do with these new learnings to make you recognizable in this world? Strive to be aware of those emotions that serve your highest good and the good of all concerned along with your God given ability to positively enhance your emotions and the emotions of those around you.

Exploring yourself in light of meaningful content, including the Holy Scriptures, gives you the opportunity to identify and adjust behavior that will improve your effectiveness in the world and opens up the doors into effective, sustainable learning and growth, along with the fullness of life Jesus died to bring you: *"I have come that you may have life and have it to the fullest"* (John 10:10).

For example, let's say you just learned three positive responses that are proven to increase effective relationships you care about. You will now explore specific behaviors that you will commit to in the coming weeks that will help you anchor those specific positive responses in those relationships.

An *explore statement* after learning content that has meaning and value at a relationship seminar would look like this. *"I commit to ask effective questions for clarity in my conversations this week and release mind-reading along with assuming I know what other people are thinking. I will practice releasing my need to be right, liked, and understood and replace that need with curious and sincere conversations."*

The L.O.V.E. Learning Circle is applied after each lesson to deepen your learnings and integrate them into your words, thoughts, deeds, and actions all in and through the Holy Spirit, our helper and counselor.

The short version of the L.O.V.E. Learning Circle as applied to the 25 Solutions: *You will have the opportunity at the end of each entry to pause, capture, and apply your Ah Ha moments:*

L: **LEARN & LISTEN:** Pause and invite the Holy Spirit into your experience of reading each lesson. Be especially attentive to content that is meaningful and adds value to your life experience both personally and professionally. What's in this verse or phrase, tip or technique that will help me anchor my identity in Christ more today than yesterday?

O: **OBSERVE:** Seek out 1–3 gold nuggets of knowledge that add value and meaning to your personal relationship with Jesus and the witness of His love through you. What sparks my attention and desire to learn more? Journal and proclaim what the Holy Spirit is saying to you as you pause on the pieces of information that capture your attention. Ask: *What specifically about this verse, insight, or technique caused me to pause and reflect? What moved me away from my fears, doubts, and worries into trust and confidence in God's presence and guidance in my life?*

V: **VISUALIZE:** Visualize integrating the meaningful verses and messages into your daily life. What do you look like, feel like, and sound like as you identify and adjust your thoughts, perceptions, and behaviors to align with the guidance and insights you have attained through your reading and time with God? Use your imagination to ignite the emotions you will feel as you visualize more of God and less of you (St. John the Baptist's Prayer: *I must decrease and He must increase.*)

E: **EXPLORE:** Explore a specific positive action step you will commit to taking in the coming days and weeks to integrate the new learnings into your words, thoughts, deeds, and actions as you resurrect your identity in Christ and move into making God recognizable in your daily thoughts, words, deeds, and actions. Explore what you will notice to be different in your life as a result of applying the insights given to you through the Holy Spirit into your day-to-day interactions personally and professionally.

# 25 Solutions to Refresh Your Identity in Christ:

**Opening Prayer:**

*Dear Lord, too often I experience identity theft that results in behavior and emotions that do not make You recognizable in this world. Forgive me for following the shiny objects that end up imprisoning me in the vicious cycle of asserting my will over Your will, my thoughts over the Holy Scriptures, and my emotions over the fruit of the Spirit: love, joy, peace, patience, kindness, goodness, and self-control.*

*"Break me free, Lord, from the sin that so easily entangles me and the yoke of slavery that restricts me in a small cocoon of fear, doubt, and worry. I want to fly with You to the places You have prepared for me to go, refresh my identity in You, Lord. Override my EGO and set me free from the prison of self: I, me, my. Remind me of whose I am. Your child, created for good works that You have prepared in advance for me to do, part of a royal priesthood, a holy nation, a people who belong to You to declare the praises of Him who called me out of darkness into this marvelous light"* (Ephesians 2:10; 1 Peter 2:9).

*Show me what is for me as I read through the entries contained in this book and give me the strength, wisdom, and courage to apply within my words, thoughts, deeds, and actions what You place upon my heart to refresh my identity in You so that I can run and not grow weary, walk and not faint, on this journey of life You have blessed me with.*

# WHAT DETERMINES THE DIRECTION OF YOUR HEART?

Your identity can be robbed by the five P's: Position, Popularity, Possessions, People, and Pace. Here we will focus on Possessions.

*"Do not store up for yourselves treasures on earth, where moth and rust destroy, and where thieves break in and steal"* (Matthew 6:19).

Jesus was talking to his disciples when he told them not to store up treasures (possessions) here on earth.

The disciples probably looked around perplexed when Jesus stated those words. They had just given up ALL their possessions and earthly treasures to come and follow Him.

Jesus, being both God and man, knew that even though they identified themselves as Christ followers and gave up their jobs they had as fisherman, businessmen, and tax collectors, they would have the tendency to slip back into their old identity behaviors.

Jesus knows our tendencies to return to our old habits.

What is in our heart dictates our habits and outcomes. What is your heart filled with?

When times get tough and we are not practicing the spiritual disciplines of God, we can begin to accumulate possessions and allow our possessions to define who we are.

Our possessions can become a great distraction that keeps us from who we ought to be in Christ.

If our old behaviors include the accumulation of possessions and stuff, what does Jesus say we should do instead?

> "But store up for yourselves treasures in heaven, where moths and vermin do not destroy, and where thieves do not break in and steal" (Matthew 6:20).

What does Jesus mean? What does storing up treasures in Heaven look like in action?

It is simple, treasure what God treasures. God treasures people not possessions. We can't take our possessions with us to Heaven. Is our identity defined by our possession or by the time we spend serving others?

It is often difficult to look into the mirror to see a true reflection of our physical bodies, and most often even harder to hold the mirror up to our souls.

What is in the heart is what drives our behaviors.

If we are not careful our identity can be identified by:
- *Accumulating stuff*
- *Taking care of stuff*
- *Maintaining the status quo of stuff*
- *Focusing on stuff*
- *Depending on stuff*
- *Comforted by stuff*

If your time is consumed by the accumulation and maintenance of possessions, then you won't have time to focus on serving people.

God is in the people business, not the possession business. God treasures people not possessions.

What do you treasure?

## Refresh Your Identity in Christ:

*"For where your treasure is, there your heart will be also"*
(Mathew 6:21).

Your heart dictates your habits and your outcomes. If you want to see if you are being identified by your possessions look at these two things.

1. Where and how do I spend my money? With my money am I advancing God's Kingdom or am I obtaining earthly possessions?
2. How am I spending my time? Am I spending my time caught up in my possessions and things or am I spending time in relationships with people?

By looking at these two activities, you can hold up that mirror to your soul and audit what is really going on internally.

The beautiful thing is that once you acknowledge what is going on, you can then change your heart, habits, and outcomes! (If it appears they need to be changed. Many should make drastic changes . . . and others not so much.)

*"But seek first his kingdom and his righteousness, and all these things will be given to you as well"* (Mathew 6:33).

*Dear God,*
*Please help me examine my heart to determine if I am storing up treasures here on earth or treasures up in Heaven. Please shine your light into those dark areas of my heart to reveal truth. Give me the discernment and awareness of putting people and relationships priority over possessions. Remind me to seek YOU first and your kingdom first daily.*

*L.O.V.E. Learning Circle: Clarity of Focus Leads to Accuracy of Response:*

L: **Learn & Listen:** What's in this verse or phrase, tip or technique that will help me anchor my identity in Christ more today than yesterday?

All my heart should be given to the Lord my God. He is my treasure. Matt 22:37

Seek you God first Matt. 6:33    Matt 6:21

O: **Observe:** My 1–3 gold nuggets I want to remember and pull into behavior:

1 Do not store up treasures on earth - possessions
2 Treasure what God treasures - people
3 How do I spend my money
   How do I spend my time

V: **Visualize:** Visualize integrating the meaningful verses and messages into your daily life. What will you notice to be different in your thoughts, perceptions, and behaviors?

I will put God and people before all the things in my life. Search my heart Lord and reveal what I am making a treasure.

E: **Explore:** Explore one specific forward action step you commit to taking in the coming days to help anchor your identity in Christ. Explore what you will notice to be different personally and professionally as you apply today's learnings.

✳ Seek God first everyday.

Psalm 139:23-24 Search me oh God and know my heart! Try me and know my thoughts! And see if there be any grievous way in me, and lead me in the way everlasting!

# HELLO MY NAME IS . . .

*". . . you will be called by a new name that the mouth of the LORD will bestow"* (Isaiah 62:2b).

Think about the last time you introduced yourself or described yourself to another person. How did you identify yourself?

I met a young lady at church the other night and she introduced herself by saying, "Hi, my name is Lisa, I am Scott and Nancy's daughter."

The way Lisa introduced herself really didn't tell me all the unique qualities and characteristics that God fashioned together when He created her. She was able to help me with my mental schemata to place her with a family, but that was just a limited introduction and didn't include important information about her personally.

I proceeded to ask her more questions and she revealed a little more. I found out that she grew up in the church and that she was actively involved in student ministry with a heart for sharing the word of God with youth.

Why did Lisa introduce herself in the way she did? Is this a societal thing, a cultural thing?

What do you say when you introduce yourself? Hello my name is . . . ?

Recently my son Jacob became a Christian and was baptized. His transformation was much like Paul's transformation.

> *"Then Saul, who also is called Paul, filled with the Holy Spirit, looked straight at Elymas . . ."* (Acts 13:9).

Jacob has struggled for many years with drug abuse.

At times as Jacob's mom, I would use these descriptions to identify my two boys. When I told people about my son Jacob, I would say things such as, "Jacob has walked a hard road, Jacob is the one who has spent time in jail, Jacob is a drug addict."

I am beyond blown away in the miracle that has taken place this year with Jacob. He has met Jesus on his own personal road to Damascus and has been transformed.

The Holy Spirit intervened and totally wiped Jacob free from his addictions by the grace of God and only through God's strength.

He still must take up his cross daily, but he is no longer a slave to his former self.

He can proudly introduce himself and say, 'I am Jacob—born again, an overcomer, transformed, anointed, abiding in Christ, and producing fruit!' Amen to that.

What we say about ourselves has power and that power has the capacity to hard wire our brains. Our thoughts and our words have the strength to shape our minds and the way we perceive ourselves.

My husband Lar lost his leg to bone cancer when he was seven years old. During those formative years as a youth, he could have used his situation to define who he was. He could have used that circumstance to define how he saw himself.

Others would define Lar as, "Lar the amputee, Lar the one-legged guy, Lar the disabled guy, Lar the cripple, etc."

Lar was beyond that. The name other's called Lar did not define him. He could have given power over to others assumptions and perceptions; however, he had to determine who he was and how he viewed himself. He was strong in his identity, because he let HIS identity define him.

He was a confident young man and knew that his physical circumstances wouldn't shape his identity. He would lean on God and listen to what God had to say about who he was.

When Lar shares his personal story with others, he often mentions that he has a daily choice when he puts his one foot on the floor in the morning to get out of bed. He decides what his mindset will be for the day. He will not allow his circumstances to determine his mindset and identity. Lar could choose to get upset about his situation; however, he makes a choice that will serve him and his creator.

Lar chooses daily to prevail! And so can you.

## Refresh Your Identity in Christ: Let Me Re-introduce Myself

Take out a sheet of paper and create two columns. In the first column, list anything that comes to your mind on how you define yourself. How do you introduce yourself?

In the second column list what God says about you. How does God view you?

| Who you say you are | Who God Says you are |
| --- | --- |
| "I am just a student." | "You are an ambassador to your biology class, you are an ambassador to your social clubs, you are an ambassador to your teachers." |
| "I am just a stay at home mom." | "You are sharing the love and truth of God, you are modeling to your children what Jesus looks like, you are forgiving, you are showing grace, you are training the next generation." |

| Who you say you are | Who God Says you are |
|---|---|
| "I am just an electrician." | "You are working unto the Lord, you are being a witness to others, you are the only Bible someone else might read." |

*Dear God,*

*Thank You for the transformation that occurs when we begin to start identifying with who You say that we are. Thank You for giving us a spirit that is the same spirit that performed countless miracles. Please help me be receptive to the spirit and listen to the quiet small voice that helps me to reintroduce myself in my true identity. Please give me discernment for when I need to click the 'refresh' button to restore my connection and true identity to my creator: God and that I can boldly introduce myself as a child of God through the saving grace of Christ's blood. In your precious name, Amen.*

*L.O.V.E. Learning Circle: Clarity of Focus Leads to Accuracy of Response:*

L: **Learn & Listen:** What's in this verse or phrase, tip or technique that will help me anchor my identity in Christ more today than yesterday?

_____

_____

_____

_____

O: **Observe:** My 1–3 gold nuggets I want to remember and pull into behavior:

_____

_____

_____

_____

V: **Visualize:** Visualize integrating the meaningful verses and messages into your daily life. What will you notice to be different in your thoughts, perceptions, and behaviors?

_____

_____

_____

_____

E: **Explore:** Explore one specific forward action step you commit to taking in the coming days to help anchor your identity in Christ. Explore what you will notice to be different personally and professionally as you apply today's learnings.

_____

_____

_____

_____

# STAND UP FOR
# YOUR IDENTITY

When the soldiers came to collect Jesus for the crucifixion, He knew why they had come yet did not shrink back from His identity:

*"Jesus, knowing all that was going to happen to Him, went out and asked them, 'Who is it you want?'... 'Jesus of Nazareth,' they replied.*

*"I am He," Jesus said . . ." (John 18:4-5).*

Have you ever found yourself face to face with accusations? A "Who did this? Or What do you believe" moment and you wanted to run and hide for fear that you would receive a negative consequence from stepping up and owning your part in the unwanted outcome or declaring your belief in Christ?

Jesus, in spite of knowing all that was going to happen to Him: the scourging, pain, deep suffering, and death, answered the soldier with confidence: *I am He.*

That is the best example of standing in your identity in the face of undesirable consequences as a result of speaking the truth about who you are, your identity in God, ever recorded in history.

Anxiety begins to dilute our sense of identity and along with it our moral convictions when we consciously consent to fear, doubt, and worry.

Stress is the power we give to outside circumstances to define what we believe we are capable of handling successfully.

When we shrink back from who we are for the sake of avoiding negative reactions, we lose focus on our purpose and mission in and through Christ.

**Refresh your identity in Christ:** To *boost your courage to declare your identity in Christ and speak truth when faced with opposition.*

Memorize the following Scriptures and declare your identity in Christ:

*"I have been crucified with Christ and I no longer live, but Christ lives in me. The life I now live in the body, I live by faith in the Son of God, Who loved me and gave himself for me"* (Galatians 2:20).

**DECLARE:** I have been crucified with Christ on the cross (my wants, cravings, and desires) I choose today to live by faith in Christ Who died to save me.

*"We are therefore Christ's ambassadors, as though God were making His appeal though us"* (2 Corinthians 5:20a).

**DECLARE:** I am Christ's ambassador and He is making His appeal for His purposes through me (too often I am my own ambassador making my appeal for me, my need to be right, liked, and understood that robs my true identity and freedom in Christ).

*"But you are a chosen people, a royal priesthood, a holy nation, God's special possession, that you may declare the praises of Him who called you out of darkness into his wonderful light"* (1 Peter 2:9).

**DECLARE:** I am chosen by God, placed in a royal priesthood, God's special possession, I am highly valued, loved, safe and protected by the King of Kings and Lord of Lords. My identity is in Christ. My purpose is to declare the praises of the One Who called me by name out of darkness into His wonderful light.

*Dear God,*
*Thank You for filling me with the grace to stand firm in the person You have called me to be in this world. When asked by others who I am and what I believe, I rejoice that I have the ability to speak with the same confidence that Jesus had in the face of adverse reactions. Help me to declare who You have created me to be with confidence in every situation that unfolds before me this week ... I am who I am.*

*L.O.V.E. Learning Circle: Clarity of Focus Leads to Accuracy of Response:*

L: **LEARN & LISTEN:** What's in this verse or phrase, tip or technique that will help me anchor my identity in Christ more today than yesterday?

_____

_____

_____

_____

O: **OBSERVE:** My 1–3 gold nuggets I want to remember and pull into behavior:

_____

_____

_____

_____

V: **VISUALIZE:** Visualize integrating the meaningful verses and messages into your daily life. What will you notice to be different in your thoughts, perceptions, and behaviors?

_____

_____

_____

E: **EXPLORE:** Explore one specific forward action step you commit to taking in the coming days to help anchor your identity in Christ. Explore what you will notice to be different personally and professionally as you apply today's learnings.

_____

_____

_____

_____

# Flip Self-Focus to Other-Focused & Joy Returns

*"Therefore, if you have any encouragement from being united with Christ, if any comfort from his love, if any common sharing in the Spirit, if any tenderness and compassion, then make my joy complete by being like-minded, having the same love, being one in spirit and of one mind. Do nothing out of selfish ambition or vain conceit. Rather, in humility value others above yourselves, not looking to your own interests but each of you to the interests of others"* (Philippians 2:1-4).

While walking along a beach, an elderly gentleman saw someone in the distance bending down, picking something up and throwing it into the ocean. As he got closer, he saw that the figure was that of a young man, picking up starfish one by one and tossing them gently back into the water. He came closer still and called out, "Good morning! May I ask what it is that you are doing?"

The young man paused, looked up, and replied, "Throwing starfish into the ocean."

The old man smiled, and said, "I must ask, then, why are you throwing starfish into the ocean?"

To this, the young man replied, "The sun is up and the tide is going out. If I don't throw them in, they'll die."

Upon hearing this, the elderly observer commented, "But, young man, do you not realize that there are miles and miles of beach and there are starfish all along every mile? You can't possibly make a difference!"

The young man listened politely. Then he bent down, picked up another starfish, and threw it into the ocean past the breaking waves and said, "It made a difference for that one."

This well-known story from an unknown author gives us the opportunity to realize the invitation we have to make a difference in another person's life. Even better if we expand these feelings to all of Nature's (God's) creatures.

Have you ever noticed that happiness returns when you shift your focus from self to another person in need?

As we choose to make a difference in the lives of people around us, regardless of how insignificant it is to onlookers, we will ignite a greater good that ripples out into humanity along with a resurrected sense of purpose beyond ourselves.

Charity is love in action for other people. Rather than overlooking an opportunity to make a small difference in another person's life, when you live a life of charity, you embrace opportunities each day to respond to people in need with your gifts, time, and talents.

When you relate to every human being through a lens of love and charity your inner dialogue sounds like this

*Dear God, show me how I can contribute to a greater good in this person's life as a result of our time together.*

As Mother Teresa said, *"We can do no great things, only little things with great love." Make a difference in another person's life today and watch the love spill over into other relationships you care about."*

Focusing on self: what I think, want and need, hijacks our true identity which is set aflame during our small acts of service fueled by love.

This week begin your day with a simple prayer:

*Dear Lord, may I be a pencil in your hand today that You may write messages of encouragement and love on the hearts of those entrusted to my care. Use my words and actions (including body language and intonation) to make You recognizable in the world. Show me whose life I can make a difference in and how I can help someone.*

*L.O.V.E. Learning Circle: Clarity of Focus Leads to Accuracy of Response:*

L: **LEARN & LISTEN:** What's in this verse or phrase, tip or technique that will help me anchor my identity in Christ more today than yesterday?

_____

_____

_____

_____

O: **OBSERVE:** My 1–3 gold nuggets I want to remember and pull into behavior:

_____

_____

_____

_____

V: **VISUALIZE:** Visualize integrating the meaningful verses and messages into your daily life. What will you notice to be different in your thoughts, perceptions, and behaviors?

_____

_____

_____

_____

E: **EXPLORE:** Explore one specific forward action step you commit to taking in the coming days to help anchor your identity in Christ. Explore what you will notice to be different personally and professionally as you apply today's learnings.

_____

_____

_____

_____

# "If" Statements that Rob

*" 'If You are the Son of God,' he said, 'throw yourself down. For it is written: 'He will command his angels concerning you, and they will lift you up in their hands, so that you will not strike your foot against a stone' "* (Matthew 4:6).

After being baptized, Jesus was led by the Spirit into the wilderness to be tempted by the devil. During Jesus' time in the desert he fasted. He fasted for forty days and forty nights.

Can you imagine how you might react being tempted by the devil after fasting for this long?

I don't know about you, but I would be HANGRY. My emotional state would override my top down thinking and I have no doubt that I wouldn't make the soundest decisions. I would want to do what was easiest and most comfortable in the moment.

However, Jesus knew what was happening and was keen to the devil's schemes. Are you keen to the devil's schemes? My prayer is to ask God to help increase my awareness of Satan's attacks, schemes, and lies in order to see clearly what is happening before me.

I can be tempted easily when I skip a meal, which usually leads to jumping out of my character that aligns with God. The devil loves when we jump out of the character that God has created us to be.

The devil tempted Jesus three times and each time Jesus resisted.

What similarity do you see between these two verses where the devil is tempting Jesus?

> ". . . *If You are the Son of God, tell these stones to become bread*" (Matthew 4:3).

> "*If You are the Son of God, throw yourself down*" (V. 6a).

The devil starts out by trying to plant a seed of doubt into Jesus' mind by questioning His true identity. "*If You are the Son of God.*"

Guess what? God already proclaimed in Matthew 3 when Jesus was baptized by John who Jesus was. Jesus was the Son of God.

> "*And a voice from heaven said, 'This is my Son, whom I love; with Him I am well-pleased'* " (Matthew 3:17).

God already declared Jesus' true identity. He was the Son of God. Period, stop, the end!

When the devil got Jesus into the desert to be tempted, he tried to plant a seed of doubt and question who Jesus truly was by saying, "If You are the Son of God." If! There is no 'If'. God had already declared who Jesus was.

Jesus did not need to prove his identity to the devil by falling into his temptation and doing what the devil suggested. Jesus knew 'who' he was and 'whose' he was.

How many times does the devil do this with us? How many times have you heard those "if" statements? *If I was thinner, If I was smarter, If I had more money, If I had more time, If I lived in a bigger house, If you loved me, If . . .*

Those "if" statements are identity robbers.

Notice when you start to say or think an "if" statement. Acknowledge that it happened or is beginning to happen and replace it with something else.

I am working towards my health.

I am uniquely made by God with specific talents only for me.

I am getting out of debt by saving monthly.

I am a good steward of my time.

I am a child of God.

I am loved by the One who died to save my life.

I am working with the gifts God has given to me.

Most often the devil doesn't start with lies, he asks questions. He began by asking Jesus a question.

We need to be prepared to state clearly who we are in Christ when the devil starts to whisper questions to us in order to place seeds of doubt.

Start proclaiming your identity in Christ by refreshing your identity by stating who you are boldly.

*Dear God, thank You for giving the gift of your discerning voice that helps me identify who I am and for the gifts You have given me. The gift of giving me your still quiet voice in times of doubt. The ability to hear You through all the external noise. The freedom You give me as I walk in your peace and grace. Please give me awareness when I begin to step out of character in Christ.*

*L.O.V.E. Learning Circle: Clarity of Focus Leads to Accuracy of Response:*

L: **LEARN & LISTEN:** What's in this verse or phrase, tip or technique that will help me anchor my identity in Christ more today than yesterday?

_____

_____

_____

_____

O: **OBSERVE:** My 1–3 gold nuggets I want to remember and pull into behavior:

_____

_____

_____

_____

V: **VISUALIZE:** Visualize integrating the meaningful verses and messages into your daily life. What will you notice to be different in your thoughts, perceptions, and behaviors?

_____

_____

_____

_____

E: **EXPLORE:** Explore one specific forward action step you commit to taking in the coming days to help anchor your identity in Christ. Explore what you will notice to be different personally and professionally as you apply today's learnings.

_____

_____

_____

_____

# MISPLACED IDENTITY: YOU ARE NOT WHO YOU WERE

*"But you are a chosen people, a royal priesthood, a holy nation, God's special possession, that you may declare the praises of him who called you out of darkness into his wonderful light"* (1 Peter 2:9).

Praise God that he has called us out of darkness and into his wonderful light.

Are you living in his wonderful light? What stops you from living in his wonderful light?

Are you listening to lies that you are telling yourself about yourself? Are you stuck in a loop of misplaced identity?

The good news is that you are not who you were!

*"Therefore, if anyone is in Christ, the new creation has come: The old has gone, the new is here!"* (2 Corinthians 5:17).

One of the easiest ways for the devil to lure you back into sin is to get you to believe that you never left. Think about the things that tempt you. Usually they are specific to you: food, drugs, alcohol, lack of exercise, cussing, and/or pornography.

The devil wants you stuck in the identity that does not glorify God.

Remember, your purpose here on earth is to bring God glory and to praise Him in everything and through everything.

The devil is not very smart and usually tempts us with the temptations that he knows will lead us to stumble and eventually fall. They are usually the same temptation offenders that usually get us hook line and sinker. However, the devil doesn't have the last say. The victory has been won by our Lord and Savior Jesus Christ.

You don't have to place your identity in those things that once held you captive and kept you from your freedom.

The devil wants to keep you in his snares and prevent your growth in Christ. He knows how powerful you can be if you are walking by the spirit and are modeling your identity through Christ-like behaviors.

> *"But now in Christ Jesus you who once were far away have been brought near by the blood of Christ"* (Ephesians 2:13).

Paul reminds the Ephesians that they too were once far away and lost in their sin. The hope that Paul encourages the Ephesians with is the same hope you have today.

You can be brought near and redeemed through grace by the blood of Jesus. The old is gone and the new has come.

You no longer have to place your identity in who you were. That misplaced identity has been buried with Christ and is now resurrected through His eternal life.

Whenever the devil says, "Look at who you were", you can now say, "Yes, I WAS, and look whose I am".

## Refresh Your Identity in Christ:

Thank God for saving me from who I was yesterday, a week ago, and a year ago!

If you are still enslaved to sin that is keeping you from God, repent with a heartfelt prayer that speaks your truth. Ask God to fill you with the Holy Spirit and to lead you away from the sins that have you ensnared.

> *Dear God, I often define who I am by who I was. I am no longer blinded and falsely accused by the ruler of this world. I know that the devil comes to steal, kill, and destroy us and our testimony. Please help me keep my feet firmly planted in truth and to build my foundation on your word. When temptation comes, please help me identify what is happening and to provide a way out. I pray that I am open to that small quiet voice that leads me closer to you. I know I am a new creation in Christ and the old is gone and the new has come. I no longer have misplaced identity. My true identity comes by your grace and Christ's blood spilled for me on the cross. I know I don't deserve any of this, however you loved us so much that you broke the heavens and came down to save us. I am forever grateful.*

*L.O.V.E. Learning Circle: Clarity of Focus Leads to Accuracy of Response:*

L: **Learn & Listen:** What's in this verse or phrase, tip or technique that will help me anchor my identity in Christ more today than yesterday?

_____

_____

_____

_____

O: **Observe:** My 1–3 gold nuggets I want to remember and pull into behavior:

_____

_____

_____

_____

V: **Visualize:** Visualize integrating the meaningful verses and messages into your daily life. What will you notice to be different in your thoughts, perceptions, and behaviors?

_____

_____

_____

_____

E: **Explore:** Explore one specific forward action step you commit to taking in the coming days to help anchor your identity in Christ. Explore what you will notice to be different personally and professionally as you apply today's learnings.

_____

_____

_____

_____

# GREED BREEDS ANXIETY & SHRINKS CONFIDENCE

*Dear Lord, open my heart and mind to your unselfish ways.*
*You served others over your own needs. You continually loved*
*in the face of hatred. May my motives be rooted in your love*
*for me for I cannot give out what I have not experienced*
*within. Help me to put to death all of the faces of greed in my*
*life. Make me aware of the tricky spots that greed hides behind*
*when it comes to my behavior. I find myself at a place of gener-*
*osity when it is convenient and fits in with my to-do list. Move*
*me to generosity with my time, assumptions, and behavior. I*
*want to make You recognizable in this world. Have your way*
*with me in spite of myself.*

*"But among you there must not be even a hint of sexual immo-*
*rality, or of any kind of impurity, or of greed, because these are*
*improper for God's holy people"* (Ephesians 5:3).

Greed is an intense and selfish desire for something, especially wealth, power, or food. The etymology of the word greed, speaks of a voracious hunger for food and/or money.

The definition of anxiety is a feeling of worry, nervousness, or unease, typically about an imminent event with potentially unfavorable effects.

Below is a real story from my journey that pulls greed (intense desire for something) and anxiety (nervousness about an imminent event of something with an uncertain outcome) together:

*"I sat in my oncologist's office as he described the potential effects of the chemotherapy I would be starting that week. One BIG FAT ramification lingered in my mind: in two weeks I was told I would lose all of my hair, possibly eyebrows/eyelashes. With hair halfway down my back this was a terrifying thought. Anxiety was roaring through my veins like a hungry lion devouring my inner peace and confidence. Why? Because I had an intense desire to keep something I might lose, so much so that it robbed me of inner freedom that comes from my soul's knowing: I am not my physical appearance and peace would return as I released this intense longing. I never realized that I was greedy for hair until I lost it."*

Now, you may say, "I don't blame you for wanting to keep your hair, I think everyone would feel that way, what's wrong with wanting that?" Nothing, until the longing starts to rob your inner peace and confidence which directly impacts how you show up in life.

Greed breeds anxiety which creates insecurities, heaviness on the heart and discontentment.

Have you ever experienced greed (a selfish and intense desire for something) resulting in anxiety (worry, nervousness that you might not get what you intensely desire) in the following areas?

- **TIME:** *An intense and selfish desire for another person's time or attention? Or greedy when it comes to your time that results in anxiety: "Stop interrupting ME . . . can't you see I am busy?" . . . that's worth reflecting on this week.*
- **POSSESSIONS:** *Comparing and envying what others have resulting in greed for more stuff? Sometimes it's as simple as greed for warm water and you are emotionally spun when it runs out because other members of the household used it all up. In the office there is plenty of earth school opportunities*

*to practice letting go of greed. Greed can wrap its bony little claws around an insatiable desire to possess responses from other people: the need to be right, liked and understood, or possess the "badge of honor", whatever that honor happens to be in the moment.*

- **POWER:** *An intense desire to control your status, popularity, and especially other people. Greed has a hay-day in this space resulting in a ton of unnecessary anxiety.*

The inner dialogue of greed sounds like: I need more (time, money, space, attention, validation); It's not enough.

Greed walks hand in hand with victimization and often results in a massive pity party.

When encountering people with physical limitations Jesus would speak to the healing and release: pick up your mat (Luke 5:24); throw off your cloak (Mark 10:50); take off the grave clothes (John 11:43).

Reflect on the following question:
- Where do you recognize greed in your life?
- Identify specific attitudes that *Edge God Out* of your behavior when it comes to being greedy with your time? Attention? Space? Money? Possessions? For example, I get greedy with my time when I have a deadline on a project. The attitude is self-centered focus. The behavior that shows up uninvited is stone walling people that interrupt me.
- Explore the following scriptures on greed and invite the Holy Spirit to adjust a specific behavior you have identified in your life that is associated with being greedy and results in anxiety.

*"Then he said to them, 'Watch out! Be on your guard against all kinds of greed; life does not consist in an abundance of possessions' " (Luke 12:15).*

*"Put to death, therefore, whatever belongs to your earthly nature: sexual immorality, impurity, lust, evil desires, and greed, which is idolatry"* (Colossians 3:5).

## Refresh Your Identity in Christ:

- Observe how the heaviness of anxiety robs your peace and confidence in Christ as a result of the serpent of greed this week. Greed slithers into your facial expressions, body language, and intonation restricting how you show up in life resulting in a heavy version of you. Look out for the ugly behavior that crashes the scene when greed is restricting your perceptions as it commonly fuels mind-reading and impoverished assumptions, not based in reality but fueled by an insatiable desire for more ... it will literally suck the life out of you and those around you.

- Nail down one behavior you can identify that shows up in the presence of greed. Write it down and run it up "Weakness Mountain" (a powerhouse technique taken from the Sherpa Process Driven Executive Coaching Program). In a nut shell: **Acknowledge** the behavior (confess it to the Lord) => **Observe** when it shows up in your behavior => **Change the behavior** (invite Jesus into the behavior and ask for the strength to replace the unwanted behavior with a behavior that aligns with your identity in Christ) => **Evaluate** (what do you notice to be different as a result of implementing the new behavior, and Christ like attitude? What are the ramifications of that intentional shift?

- Invite the Holy Spirit into your anxiety flare ups this week. Notice if greed is playing a role when it comes to having an intense desire for something to be a certain way. For example, you start a project and get interrupted by someone who needs a piece of information that only you have access to. Notice if anxiety kicks in and along with-it ugly behavior. If this is the case know that greed for time and space is at play. This exercise does not negate the importance of healthy boundaries rather it is to bring attention to the antics of greed in daily life and the anxiety it produces. Generosity is a worthy character trait to explore in the face of greedy flare ups in life.

*Dear God, those who give generously of their time, talents, and treasure in life will prosper and be refreshed (Proverbs 11:25). Perhaps the prosperity that You speak of comes in the form of profound peace, contentment, and joy. I give You permission to sift my interior world and reveal to me the strongholds of greed that create undue anxiety and stress in my life. I am nothing without You. Greed comes from feeling that I do not have enough of something, therefore an intense selfish desire for it begins to overtake my moral compass and I find myself occupying the space of selfish ambitions (Philippians 2:3) and sleepless nights. Override me Lord for your purposes. Remind my mind that in You I lack nothing. Move me to go for what You have tasked me to do in life 100% and be attached to nothing but You; my heart in your heart, my will consumed by yours. Get thee behind me greed, I am a child of God.*

*L.O.V.E. Learning Circle: Clarity of Focus Leads to Accuracy of Response:*

L: **LEARN & LISTEN:** What's in this verse or phrase, tip or technique that will help me anchor my identity in Christ more today than yesterday?

_____

_____

_____

_____

O: **OBSERVE:** My 1–3 gold nuggets I want to remember and pull into behavior:

_____

_____

V: **VISUALIZE:** Visualize integrating the meaningful verses and messages into your daily life. What will you notice to be different in your thoughts, perceptions, and behaviors?

_____

_____

_____

_____

E: **EXPLORE:** Explore one specific forward action step you commit to taking in the coming days to help anchor your identity in Christ. Explore what you will notice to be different personally and professionally as you apply today's learnings.

_____

_____

_____

_____

# A KEY TO FREEDOM YOU WANT TO KNOW

*". . . for people are slaves to whatever has mastered them"* (2 Peter 2:19).

As you reflect on your own relationship with the world, what has mastered you in your life? Is it your environment? Opinions and reactions of other people? The need to be seen, acknowledged, and recognized? Power over others? The need to be liked, right, or understood?

Is it your behavior? My clients, who are seeking freedom from compulsive behavior, will often say, "I just can't help myself." This reveals a type of personal enslavement due to allowing some food, substance, situation, or person to master them over time, which in some cases results in a biological addiction and a leak in one's identity to an external force.

Whenever you give power over to an exterior element you render yourself vulnerable to rising and falling depending upon how that element shows up in your life leading to emotional and even physical disability.

The stress hormone is linked directly to your emotional state of mind and heart. Extended emotional stress often leads to personal enslavement, which usually walks hand in hand with unhealthy outlets.

The key to freedom in situations like this lies in your ability to accept where you are at, accompanied by a desire for positive personal transformation and a choice to take steps in that direction.

Dannemiller's formula for change offers food for reflection and personal empowerment: D x V x F x L > R. **Dissatisfaction** with your current situation or circumstance times a clear **Vision** of what you want times **Forward** action steps (clarity of focus leads to accuracy of response) times effective **Leadership** acumen MUST be greater than your **Resistance** in order for positive, effective, and lasting change to occur (this can be applied to individual and team goals and initiatives).

## Refresh Your Identity in Christ:

As you seek freedom in Christ this week perhaps you can pause and identify those areas within your own life that hold you back from personal excellence, high integrity, and leadership effectiveness within your own life. You can't give out in this world what you do not take time to develop with the guidance of the Holy Spirit within your interior life.

Explore the following mindful prayer and add in your specific vices that have restricted the highest version of you:

> *Dear God, I choose this week to align my thoughts, words, and deeds with my highest good and the good of all concerned. Through the power of the Holy Spirit I ignite my ability to choose my responses to life remembering that I hold the key to victimization and empowerment. What I chose to think about sets in motion my reality. I am willing to take an honest look at those exterior elements in my own life which do not support the highest version of who I am committed to being in this world and the highest good of all concerned. Grant me the grace to take a step in the direction of release and restoration this week along with the ability to tune into the necessary resources needed to support my intention for interior freedom from exterior vices.*

*Help me to step back from worldly ways and reactions and refresh my identity in You.*

*All things are possible for me, shrinking back and allowing myself to be burdened by the yoke of slavery to unhealthy masters is not how You created me to show up in this life. I choose You and all things good, right, true, beautiful, and praiseworthy.*

*L.O.V.E. Learning Circle: Clarity of Focus Leads to Accuracy of Response:*

L: **LEARN & LISTEN:** What's in this verse or phrase, tip or technique that will help me anchor my identity in Christ more today than yesterday?

_____

_____

_____

_____

O: **OBSERVE:** My 1–3 gold nuggets I want to remember and pull into behavior:

_____

_____

_____

_____

V: **VISUALIZE:** Visualize integrating the meaningful verses and messages into your daily life. What will you notice to be different in your thoughts, perceptions, and behaviors?

_____

_____

_____

E: **EXPLORE:** Explore one specific forward action step you commit to taking in the coming days to help anchor your identity in Christ. Explore what you will notice to be different personally and professionally as you apply today's learnings.

_____

_____

_____

_____

# MUGGED BY THE MIRROR

*"You shall not covet your neighbor's house. You shall not covet your neighbor's wife, or his male or female servant, his ox or donkey, or anything that belongs to your neighbor"* (Exodus 20:17).

Y‍ou shall not covet the fake eyelashes that others wear.

The above verse slapped me in the face as I took stock and inventory of this past year.

I realized I was mugged by the mirror of my own image as I coveted other's fake eyelashes. Yes, I said fake eyelashes. I am not here to judge but to speak from my own personal experience.

I got caught up in the fake eyelash craze and became a bit obsessed with what I saw in the mirror based on what I saw on social media.

My identity last year was defined by long, thick, full volume eyelashes!

Some people live in a trivial imaged obsessed culture connected by available, instant, 24/7 communication.

I just did a quick Google search and found an article titled, "60+ Social Networking Sites You Need to Know About in 2018." That is a lot of sites that are mostly dedicated to posting pictures of "your best self", "the highlight reels of your life", and "images you want others to see".

This distorted lens through which we view the world often robs us by the "suit of comparison". Most often we determine our worth and put on our "identity suit" through the comparison lens and covet what others have.

We live in an imaged obsessed culture and it's only getting worse. The images that are projected to us have us believe what we are seeing is reality, these distorted and Photoshopped images lead us to believe they are real.

Most images and marketing ploys call us to preserve outward appearances where God is concerned inwardly. What does our heart look like? Are we just as concerned about what is going on inside our eternal bodies as we are about what is going on outside with our external appearances?

We get mired in the messages of societal culture and mugged by the mirror which can rob us of our identity and lead us to ponder if we "belong here" at all. Do I belong in this group? Or on this team? Or around this table? Or presenting in front of these people?

## Refresh Your Identity in Christ:

Taking an inventory of the last three months of your life is always helpful. Take time to **PAUSE** to see what has crept in to mug you of misaligned priorities which fuel identity distortions:

P: **PRIORITIES:** Create a list of priorities that have been a main focus these past three months.

A: **ASK:** Ask yourself, do these priorities align with my true identity and what God has for me as I live out my purpose here on earth?

U: **UNDERSTAND:** Take time to pray and understand what the driver behind these misaligned priorities has been.

S: **SEEK:** Seek God's plan for what you place value on and prayerfully ask for God's strength to realign what is true.

E: **EVALUATE:** Be gentle with yourself as you are going through the journey of life. Take time to check back in with yourself and evaluate how you are doing. Is anything creeping in that you are coveting or mugged by the mirror?

> *Dear God, please give me the wisdom and knowledge to know who I am in You. This day, give me eyes to see, a heart to feel, and a brain to discern my true identity in You. Please grant me peace and assurance that I belong here right where I am today.*
>
> *In Jesus' name, Amen.*

*L.O.V.E. Learning Circle: Clarity of Focus Leads to Accuracy of Response:*

L: **LEARN & LISTEN:** What's in this verse or phrase, tip or technique that will help me anchor my identity in Christ more today than yesterday?

_____

_____

_____

_____

O: **OBSERVE:** My 1–3 gold nuggets I want to remember and pull into behavior:

_____

_____

_____

V: **VISUALIZE:** Visualize integrating the meaningful verses and messages into your daily life. What will you notice to be different in your thoughts, perceptions, and behaviors?

_____

_____

_____

E: **EXPLORE:** Explore one specific forward action step you commit to taking in the coming days to help anchor your identity in Christ. Explore what you will notice to be different personally and professionally as you apply today's learnings.

_____

_____

_____

_____

# WHO IS THE REAL YOU?

*"Then God said, 'Let us make human beings in our image, in our likeness, so that they may rule over the fish in the sea and the birds in the sky, over the livestock and all the wild animals, and over all the creatures that move along the ground.'*

*So, God created human beings in his own image, in the image of God he created them; male and female he created them"* (Genesis 1: 26–27).

Who is the real you? Is it the image you have "filtered" for your social media site, or the unfiltered image that has been untouched?

They are both organically you; however, which one represents your truest self? Which one does the culture reward? Nobody cares about your before picture, that is your everyday look. You are never putting that picture on social media for the world to see.

The beauty and personal-care industry is an 80 billion dollar industry that appeals to your outward image and the preservation of that image.

Americans spend 80 billion dollars per year on beauty and personal care. Those statistics don't include all the other designer things we adorn our bodies with.

What we see advertised before us rarely matches who we are as individuals. Most of the models that are displayed are much fitter than the averages seen in our culture for both males and females. We then internalize these projected, most often Photoshopped images, compare ourselves against what we see and then feel "less than" and question "how do we fit in?"

How do we get our true identity back? It sounds so simple looking at the next bolded sentence on this page. **The inside of you has much more power to define you than the outside.**

Go back to the Bible to see what it says about you. *You are created in the image of God* (Genesis 1:26–27).

What does it mean that we are made in the image of God? Where is that image found? How is that image seen?

Genesis 2:7 states that Man is created by God and he is an empty dead shell. Dead body, no activity. God breathed into Adam and at that point he became a living being. God's image was imparted into Adam.

God's image is inside of us. We become physical bodies and God's image can be found in our souls. We are spiritual beings having physical experiences.

## Refresh Your Identity in Christ:

Slow down and realize you are created in the image of God. No other creature resembles God's image. When you begin to understand what this means, you can confidently represent yourself to the world without any filters. You can confidently know who you are in Christ.

Acknowledge when doubts begin to fill your mind, cast them out and proclaim out loud whose you are and who you are!

Next time you post that picture on social media ask yourself, is this edifying, serving our Lord and Savior, helping someone else, leading others to Christ?

*Dear God, as I navigate life, help me to focus on what my true reflection should be. Help in all areas where I might get caught up in outward appearances. Thank You for being more concerned with my heart, my interior world. Please help me today to examine all areas of my heart to see what's really going on. Where exactly am I placing the focus on my life? How does that show up when it comes to what I choose to spend my time doing? Please shine a light and reveal to me today what is of true value and important in light of eternity. Help me to want what You want me to have in order to refresh my identity in You.*

*L.O.V.E. Learning Circle: Clarity of Focus Leads to Accuracy of Response:*

L: **LEARN & LISTEN:** What's in this verse or phrase, tip or technique that will help me anchor my identity in Christ more today than yesterday?

_____

_____

_____

_____

O: **OBSERVE:** My 1–3 gold nuggets I want to remember and pull into behavior:

_____

_____

_____

_____

V: **VISUALIZE:** Visualize integrating the meaningful verses and messages into your daily life. What will you notice to be different in your thoughts, perceptions and behaviors?

_____

_____

_____

E: **EXPLORE:** Explore one specific forward action step you commit to taking in the coming days to help anchor your identity in Christ. Explore what you will notice to be different personally and professionally as you apply today's learnings.

_____

_____

_____

_____

# How to Recognize Pride vs. a Prideful Nature

*True Pride*:

T rue pride that has its way in you is unable to hear and respond to the voice of humility. Therefore, it has an insatiable desire to dominate, be seen, acknowledged, and recognized. True pride is blinded by self-importance over service and compassion for others. It trades in remorse and repentance for blaming, complaining, and justifying ugly and defensive behaviors.

This pride is easily frustrated and anger flares up when its plans are thwarted and people stand in its way of getting what it wants.

It is fueled by unbridled ambition that puts things before people. The non-essential before the essential and will do anything, often void of moral conscious, to get what it wants.

This pride is like a spoiled child and is seldom content or deeply satisfied . . . always wanting more.

*A Spiritually Discerning Person with a Prideful Nature:*
Know this: Even as a human being seeking to love, serve, and honor God you will experience prideful flare-ups.

The difference between a person who lives in service of pride and one who seeks to put God's ways of love and service first and experiences occasional moments of prideful flare-ups is this:

As soon as pride shows up the spiritually discerning person will feel the burn of whatever action, thought, or word associated with the prideful moment within their biology.

Feeling the discomfort this person will choose to return to God as quickly as possible; Identifying and adjusting their thoughts, words, and deeds to keep themselves aligned with the higher good of all concerned, which flows from their intimacy with God.

The spiritually discerning person sees pride for what it is and seeks the higher ground of humility, love, and gratitude. They are also able to forgive others when they have prideful moments.

Basically, the truly prideful person is enslaved to pride as they continually choose it over the ways of their godly nature.

## Refresh Your Identity in Christ:

*Solutions to overcome pride with humility:*
The person who has a prideful nature or tendency as humans do, yet is not a proud person, is one who rejects prideful flare-ups and quickly makes amends as they choose God over their prideful moment.

This week observe your behavior when other people get acknowledged, noticed, or praised over you. Pause and pray for the grace of humility to rejoice in other people's successes over your own. This results in the true freedom you ultimately seek which gives birth to joy based on your association with the servant heart of Christ within you.

Begin again, and again, and again with even more congruency today than yesterday.

Align your actions with your God given natural state of being: filling your responses to life with love, joy, peace, patience, goodness, gentleness, and self-control.

Authentic transformation beings with ruthless honesty and the ability to adjust.

> *Sweet Jesus, I give You permission to calm the Kraken of pride in my life. Too often my need to be seen, acknowledged, recognized, approved of, understood, and validated overrides my moral compass and I find myself face to face with ugly behavior as I kick and scream to defend the territory, I think is rightly mine. I find myself mucking around in lights off behavior trying to prove my worth and value to the world. Wake me up today to the truth that I am enough because You died to save my soul. Anything good in my life comes from You. I own nothing except for my ability to choose You in all things. Help me to return to humility and confidence in You quicker today than yesterday.*

*L.O.V.E. Learning Circle: Clarity of Focus Leads to Accuracy of Response:*

L: **LEARN & LISTEN:** What's in this verse or phrase, tip or technique that will help me anchor my identity in Christ more today than yesterday?

_____

_____

_____

_____

O: **OBSERVE:** My 1–3 gold nuggets I want to remember and pull into behavior:

_____

_____

_____

_____

V: **VISUALIZE:** Visualize integrating the meaningful verses and messages into your daily life. What will you notice to be different in your thoughts, perceptions, and behaviors?

_____

_____

_____

_____

E: **EXPLORE:** Explore one specific forward action step you commit to taking in the coming days to help anchor your identity in Christ. Explore what you will notice to be different personally and professionally as you apply today's learnings.

_____

_____

_____

_____

# THREE IDENTITY BUSTERS

*"Do not love the world or anything in the world. If you love the world, love for the Father is not in you. For everything in the world—the cravings of sinful people, the lust of their eyes and their boasting about what they have and do—comes not from the Father but from the world. The world and its desires pass away, but whoever does the will of God lives forever"* (1 John 2:15–17).

D o you ever have cravings, lust, or boast in life? Know that the fuel behind these emotional experiences does not flow from your soul's connection with God but from outside distractions that cause you to forget that you are a spiritual being having a physical experience.

When we begin to love things over God, unhealthy attachments begin to develop. The thing about attachments is that they are seldom content, like a spoiled child they continue to crave more of that which can never fully satisfy, leaving you wallowing in a pit of discontentment.

The other day a client was marveling at the fact that when they finally got the car they had always longed for in life, they were not any happier than they were before they got the car. Why? Because desire passes away as quickly as it enters in our interior world.

An attachment is an emotional state of clinging due to the belief that without something, situation, or outcome you cannot be happy. It is quickly followed up with the fear that you will lose that to which you are now attached to, or the astonishment that you are no happier because of it.

An unbridled desire to satisfy an unfulfilled emotional state of being or compromised self-image will often manifest in the following:

**CRAVINGS:** *an intense yearning for something...a desire...a feeling that comes along with an unsatisfied state.*

**LUST:** *a self-absorbed desire for a certain thing, person, or experience.*

**BOASTING:** *to speak with exaggeration about yourself in a prideful manner.*

## Refresh Your Identity in Christ:

When we forget to spend time daily nurturing our relationship with God, along with the things that we will draw unto ourselves at the sunset of this life, we start to wander out into the world to experience quick hits of satisfaction that leave us empty and unsatisfied. This unhealthy cycle causes us to crave more of that which can never fully satisfy: recognition, acknowledgment, status, and material things.

Increase your experience with God each day by spending time focused on what you value and love most in life...these are the things that are void of the need to define, own, control, or possess (exchange of love, watching a sunset, playing, laughing). Life is created for us to experience and grow in our ability to love and be loved. When you remember that your identity is as a child of God to give glory to God then peace will return.

Clarity of focus leads to accuracy of response and ups your ability to unzip and step out of unhealthy cravings, lusts, and boasting in life.

**KNOW WHOSE YOU ARE:** Who am I? A child of the living God, created in the image and likeness of God: *"But you are a chosen priesthood, a holy nation, God's special possession . . ."* (1 Peter 2:9a).

**KNOW WHY YOU ARE HERE:** Why am I here? To give glory to God . . . *"that you may declare the praises of him who called you out of darkness into his wonderful light"* (1 Peter 2:9b).

> *"We are therefore Christ's ambassadors, as though God were making his appeal through us. We implore you on Christ's behalf: Be reconciled to God"* (2 Corinthians 5:20).

**KNOW WHY IT MATTERS:**

> *"Be merciful to those who doubt; save others by snatching them from the fire;"* (Jude 1:22–23a).

> *"In the same way, let your light shine before others, that they may see your good deeds and glorify your Father in heaven"* (Matthew 5:16).

> *Dear God, the world and its desires pass away yet I find that I too often lose my identity in the shiny objects around me. I crave, lust, and boast about trinkets that distract me from my one desire that brings the peace and confidence I seek: to do your will. Help me today to desire one thing: to love You with all of my heart, mind, soul, and strength. I know I can't give out what I don't receive within. Fill me with an expansive aware-ness of how much You love and adore me. Lord, You have the words of eternal life, forgive me for seeking the living (eternal ways) among the dead (worldly ways).*

*L.O.V.E. Learning Circle: Clarity of Focus Leads to Accuracy of Response:*

L: **LEARN & LISTEN:** What's in this verse or phrase, tip or technique that will help me anchor my identity in Christ more today than yesterday?

———————————————————————————

———————————————————————————

_____

_____

O: **OBSERVE:** My 1–3 gold nuggets I want to remember and pull into behavior:

_____

_____

_____

_____

V: **VISUALIZE:** Visualize integrating the meaningful verses and messages into your daily life. What will you notice to be different in your thoughts, perceptions and behaviors?

_____

_____

_____

_____

E: **EXPLORE:** Explore one specific forward action step you commit to taking in the coming days to help anchor your identity in Christ. Explore what you will notice to be different personally and professionally as you apply today's learnings.

_____

_____

_____

_____

# POLLUTED POSITION

*"Once when Jacob was cooking stew, Esau came in from the open country, famished. He said to Jacob, 'Quick, let me have some of that red stew! I'm famished!' (That is why he was also called Edom.)*

*"Jacob replied, 'First sell me your birthright.'*

*"'Look, I am about to die,' Esau said. 'What good is the birthright to me?'*

*"But Jacob said, 'Swear to me first!' So he swore an oath to him, selling his birthright to Jacob.*

*"Then Jacob gave Esau some bread and some lentil stew. He ate and drank, and then got up and left. So Esau despised his birthright"* (Genesis 25:29–34).

Esau and Jacob were twin brothers. Esau was born before Jacob so that entitled Esau to the family birthright.

One day, Esau was out working and came back completely famished (hangry) and exhausted. He begged his brother Jacob to give him some stew that he had prepared. Jacob pondered this request for a bit and then asked Esau to sell his birthright in exchange for a meal.

What, wait a minute, Esau was compromising his identity, his position for a bowl of lentils?

This temporary pleasure cost him his birthright and this trade eventually transferred the lineage of Jesus Christ over to Jacob who became Israel from the House of David, which Jesus Christ was born.

There you have it. For a pot of stew, poor, hungry Esau sold his birthright. Such crass behavior would be a little like selling your wedding ring for a hamburger because you had not eaten all day, only worse.

It tells of Esau's attitude toward the things of God; His purpose and His will. It shows a lack of reverence and respect. It shows the same thing we see in too many people today when it comes to how little they regard the Lord and their identity and position in Him.

How many times do you pollute your position for temporary gain?

Perhaps it's hard for you to imagine how someone could do this, however if you stop to think about Esau and Jacob's situation, how many times have you traded or compromised something in your life that compromises your birthright in Christ?

What do you do when you are exhausted in life both spiritually, physically, and emotionally? Do you compromise your identity for temporary satisfaction?

Emotions are important and you should pay attention to how you are feeling; however, feelings are fleeting. They are temporary. Allow your feelings to be indicators and not dictators of your behavior.

What is your bowl of lentils you have compromised?

> "See that no one is sexually immoral, or is godless like Esau, who for a single meal sold his inheritance rights as the oldest son" (Hebrews 12:16).

According to this verse in the New Testament, Esau was immoral, and lacked concern for pleasing God. His spiritual blessings and responsibilities meant nothing to him. The Lord tells us to be sure we are not like Esau in this, that there be no immoral or godless person like Esau, who sold his own birthright for a single meal.

What are you farming your identity out to? Is it position, popularity, possessions, people, pace?

## Refresh Your Identity in Christ:

The world rushes today, giving little thought to God and His daily purpose for each of our lives. We are children of God. Let us never forget, not for an hour, that God and His promises are holy. He expects our lives to reflect that awareness.

Reflect on your inheritance in Christ and consider its great value to you.

Consider your "'bowl of lentils'" and identify your feelings. Are your feelings indicators to what is going on in your life, or are you allowing your feelings to dictate your actions?

> *Dear God, thank You for our birthright as co-heirs to eternity. Please open my eyes to any areas in my life where I am farming out my identity in You for position and security in this life. Help me live this life in light of eternity. There will be a great day when I will stand before You giving an account for my life. I pray that I don't take my birthright for granted and that I can live according to this great gift You have given me! My birthright anchors my identity in You . . . I lack nothing in You.*

*L.O.V.E. Learning Circle: Clarity of Focus Leads to Accuracy of Response:*

L: **LEARN & LISTEN:** What's in this verse or phrase, tip or technique that will help me anchor my identity in Christ more today than yesterday?

_____

_____

_____

_____

O: **OBSERVE:** My 1–3 gold nuggets I want to remember and pull into behavior:

_____

_____

_____

_____

V: **VISUALIZE:** Visualize integrating the meaningful verses and messages into your daily life. What will you notice to be different in your thoughts, perceptions and behaviors?

_____

_____

_____

_____

E: **EXPLORE:** Explore one specific forward action step you commit to taking in the coming days to help anchor your identity in Christ. Explore what you will notice to be different personally and professionally as you apply today's learnings.

_____

_____

_____

_____

# Aroma: What is Your Scent?

*"and walk in the way of love, just as Christ loved us and gave Himself up for us as a fragrant offering and a sacrifice to God"* (Ephesians 5:2).

There are approximately 64 verses in the Bible that contain the word aroma.

Aroma is a funny word to say. According to Webster's dictionary, the meaning of aroma is: a *distinctive, pervasive, and usually pleasant or savory smell.*

How many times have you walked into someone's house and have smelled an aroma that is unique to that house?

When people walk into your house, they smell an aroma that is unique to your house.

Over time, we have become so familiar with our "house'" aroma that we can no longer smell the aroma.

People "carry" their "house" aroma with them wherever they go.

This recently happened to me. My mom and dad came to visit and the aroma of their house came with them! I was very familiar with this unique smell once I moved out of the house.

Our unique house smell was that of must! I grew up with a damp basement and the musty basement odor would permeate the house, our clothing, and any other material it could seep into.

I remember one day in school someone asking me, "what is that smell?" I had become so accustomed to the aroma that I could no longer smell our house scent. And let me tell you, it was not a sweet aroma.

Isn't that crazy that we can be identified by our scent, our aroma?

Diving deeper into this concept of aroma, what is your scent? What aroma do you leave behind once you have left the room?

Is your aroma pleasing to the Lord? Is your aroma identified and deeply rooted in Christ?

> *"For we are to God the pleasing aroma of Christ among those who are being saved and those who are perishing. To the one we are an aroma that brings death; to the other, an aroma that brings life. And who is equal to such a task?"* (2 Corinthians 2:15-16).

I would venture to say that if there are 64 Bible verses pertaining to aroma that God cares about our aroma.

Is your identity a sweet, pleasing smell to our Lord and Savior and to those around you?

Is your aroma offensive?

## Refresh Your Identity in Christ:

As Christians, we carry a sweet fragrance of Christ in our hearts. We are invited to spread this aroma to the uttermost part of the earth.

Allow your aroma to spread forth around the world.

Think about a time that you walked into a beautifully scented garden, a fragrant bakery, or walked along the shoreline after a fresh rain. This heightened sense of smell stays with you forever and you can remember the moment and the smell. You are now able to recognize that scent wherever you go.

When you are interacting with others, whether they are Christ followers or not, are you carrying the sweet aroma of Jesus Christ with you? This aroma is reflected in your facial expressions, your intonations, and body language. It's reflected in all you do and say.

Let the fragrance of Christ rub off on people positively throughout your life.

> *Dear God, please help me today to be a sweet and pleasant aroma to You and to others as I go about my interactions. Please help me become aware when my aroma is not pleasing to You. Help me today identify those along my path who need the sweet aroma of Jesus. Guide my feet along the path You have set before me. Thank You, Jesus, for being a beautiful model of what a sweet aroma looks like, feels like, and sound like. Smells trigger memories. Replace any unpleasant memories and false beliefs about myself from my past with the sweet aroma of your healing grace so that moving forward, my identity is refreshed and restored in You. Amen!*

*L.O.V.E. Learning Circle: Clarity of Focus Leads to Accuracy of Response:*

L: **LEARN & LISTEN:** What's in this verse or phrase, tip or technique that will help me anchor my identity in Christ more today than yesterday?

_____

_____

_____

_____

O: **OBSERVE:** My 1–3 gold nuggets I want to remember and pull into behavior:

_____

_____

_____

_____

V: **VISUALIZE:** Visualize integrating the meaningful verses and messages into your daily life. What will you notice to be different in your thoughts, perceptions and behaviors?

_____

_____

_____

_____

E: **EXPLORE:** Explore one specific forward action step you commit to taking in the coming days to help anchor your identity in Christ. Explore what you will notice to be different personally and professionally as you apply today's learnings.

_____

_____

_____

_____

# FLIP REJECTION
# INTO DIRECTION

*"For the Spirit God gave us does not make us timid, but gives us POWER, Love and Self-discipline" (2 Timothy 1:7, emphasis mine).*

One of my favorite reminders of who I am in this world comes from the above verse. Let's dismantle this a little to give it more clarity of focus thus increasing our ability to put it into daily action.

First of all, know what you are and what you are not. This releases inner anxiety instantly.

**You are** a child of God, possessing the blueprint of the creator of the universe flowing through your spirit that is beyond all momentary troubles and tribulations. Your spirit knows itself to be enough, capable and victorious at all times even in the eye of the storm. Simply put, you are first and foremost a spiritual being having a physical experience as proclaimed by the Christian mystics throughout history.

**You are not** your circumstance; judgments from yourself and others; traumatic situations; rejection; fear; doubt or worry... unless you choose to believe you are in which case the spirit of fear will twist the reality of who you are as created in the image AND likeness of God.

*For God did not give us a spirit of fear but of POWER, Love, and Self-Control.*

You have a spirit that moves with self-control: the ability to choose a certain response to life that serves your well-being and the well-being of all concerned.

We do not use the spirit of self-control enough in our daily lives as we play victim to our circumstances: "If I don't get this certain outcome, I won't be able to handle it" . . . "life is a struggle" . . . "I can't do that" . . . "Nothing ever works out for me" . . . "I don't understand why they did that, said that, didn't do that . . . why things work out for other people and not for me."

In order to experience the POWER and the LOVE contained at the heart of our spirit which fuels our ability to create, self-control needs to be resurrected to the front lines of our responses to people, things, and circumstances.

Special attention should be paid to feelings of rejection, which result from not feeling good enough about your performance, behavior or self-worth.

When we feel a sense of rejection, we are disconnected from our soul's knowing that with God we lack nothing. Through Christ, with Christ, and in Christ we are always enough. Why? Because Jesus Christ is the ultimate atoning sacrifice for our inadequacies and sinful nature. As Jesus said on the cross before His spirit left his body: "It is finished." Your feelings of rejection come from forgetting that you are enough in Christ.

## Refresh Your Identity in Christ:

This week practice **self-control** . . . step back from your quick responses to life, often fueled by emotional flare-ups of unbridled ambition and seek the wisdom that flows from the Holy Spirit, known as the Counselor: *"Holy Spirit give me the words to speak that are in my best interest and reflect the higher good I am created for, or the silence needed for even greater wisdom and guidance."*

Remember, true greatness comes through the archway of temperance, humility, and love. The gap, which allows wisdom to drop in between what happens around you and your response to it, grows bigger with each act of **self-control**.

Self-control over the labels you place on other people as well as yourself when it comes to impoverished conclusions based on mind-reading and storytelling ... ask questions for clarity and separate the person from the issue at hand, seek out the facts.

> *When you feel rejected simply say: It's not rejection, it's simply direction. God uses everything for an ultimate good as I love and trust in the Lord"* (Romans 8:28).

Choose one of the following verses and commit it to memory. Pull it up from memory and declare it in the face of a perceived moment that you label as rejection:

- *"For the Spirit God gave us does not make us timid, but gives us POWER, Love, and Self-discipline" [emphasis mine]* (2 Timothy 1:7).
- *"... be transformed by the renewing of your mind"* (Romans 12:2).
- *"Finally, brothers and sisters, whatever is true, whatever is noble, whatever is right, whatever is pure, whatever is lovely, whatever is admirable—if anything is excellent or praiseworthy—think about such things"* (Philippians 4:8).
- *" 'Not by might nor by power, but by my Spirit,' says the LORD Almighty"* (Zechariah 4:6).

*Dear God, I give You permission to resurrect within me the spirit that is my birth right as your child on earth: A spirit of POWER, LOVE, and SELF-CONTROL. In order for me to experience the **power** of your **love** through my thoughts, words, and responses to the life in front of my face I need the grace of faith in action manifested through **self-control**. Help me to remember who I am this week, why I do what I do, and the bigger picture in life. Expand my ability to control my thoughts of self-defeat, judgment of self, and others that rendered me incapable of accessing the strength and power of my spirit to overcome and powerfully witness to the successful creative nature* *that manifests a greater good on earth, which I am willing to consider I will focus on at the sunset of this life. Help me to live my life backwards...doing, saying, creating those things that at my last breath, as I reflect on how I showed up each day, will cause me to hear the sweet words of ultimate success in life: " Well done, my good and faithful servant, you remembered who you are, what you are capable of & why, with the gift of each new dawn your heart continued to beat."*

*L.O.V.E. Learning Circle: Clarity of Focus Leads to Accuracy of Response:*

L: **LEARN & LISTEN:** What's in this verse or phrase, tip or technique that will help me anchor my identity in Christ more today than yesterday?

_____

_____

_____

_____

O: **OBSERVE:** My 1–3 gold nuggets I want to remember and pull into behavior:

_____

_____

_____

_____

V: **VISUALIZE:** Visualize integrating the meaningful verses and messages into your daily life. What will you notice to be different in your thoughts, perceptions and behaviors?

_____

_____

_____

E: **EXPLORE:** Explore one specific forward action step you commit to taking in the coming days to help anchor your identity in Christ. Explore what you will notice to be different personally and professionally as you apply today's learnings.

_____

_____

_____

_____

# LIVE W.O.W.

*"The mind controlled by the sinful nature is death, but the mind controlled by the Spirit is life and peace. The sinful mind is hostile to God; it does not submit to God's law, nor can it do so. Those controlled by the sinful nature cannot please God.*

*"You, however, are not controlled by the sinful nature but are in the Spirit, if indeed the Spirit of God lives in you. And if anyone does not have the Spirit of Christ, they do not belong to Christ. But if Christ is in you, then even though your body is subject to death because of sin, the Spirit gives life because of righteousness. And if the Spirit of Him who raised Jesus from the dead is living in you, He who raised Christ from the dead will also give life to your mortal bodies because of his Spirit who lives in you"* (Romans 8:6–11).

W.O.W. **W**ithin **O**mnipresent **W**onder. When you find yourself swept up in the wonder of God's omnipresence (present in all places at all times) you remember *whose* you are and pick up the trials of this world like a child's toy.

Heaviness in life is the result of a mind driven by the need to know how things are going to turn out and why things happen as they do, fear overcomes trust.

The flesh is a thief that continually steals your joy, peace, and confidence in Christ. The love of God resurrects and recovers the pieces of you that spill out into the world along the way due to fear, self-doubt, and worry.

Your place of empowerment lies in your ability to remember that you have the mind of Christ. When your mind is governed (controlled, influenced, or regulated) by the Spirit the result is life.

When your mind is governed by the flesh, the result is the death of your confidence, self-worth, courage, and power to overcome.

Jesus' words found in John 10:10 speak of the one who twists the mind and steals the identity of humanity: "The devil comes to kill and destroy but I have come that you may have life to the fullest." How does the devil kill and destroy? By poisoning the mind with falsity.

Zach Williams nailed this principle when he wrote the popular Christian song: **"Fear is a Liar"** (excerpt below):

> *When he told you you're not good enough*
> *When he told you you're not right*
> *When he told you you're not strong enough*
> *To put up a good fight*
> *When he told you you're not worthy*
> *When he told you you're not loved*
> *When he told you you're not beautiful*
> *That you'll never be enough*
> *Fear, he is a liar*
> *He will take your breath*
> *Stop you in your steps*
> *Fear he is a liar*
> *He will rob your rest*
> *Steal your happiness*
> *Cast your fear in the fire*
> *'Cause fear he is a liar*

It is also important to reflect upon Jesus' comparison to children when He referenced the kingdom of God. If we really want to enter God's kingdom of love, purpose, and freedom in Christ we must master the mind. We are not alone in this journey for whatever God calls us to master, He also offers the strength, wisdom and guidance to do it (1 Thessalonians 5:24).

Children are in the W.O.W. experience of God, the younger they are, the more predominant it is. They live within the Omnipresent Wonder of God. With curiosity and fascination within the present moment, they believe and therefore, create quickly and creatively whatever they imagine, as a result of belief, trust, and confidence in the possible. *"You of little faith, why did you doubt?"* (Matthew 14:31).

When you ask a young child if they think something is possible, they will most often respond with, "Of course it is," and then start imagining how to make the possible happen. The younger the child is, the quicker the focus is on the possible. Perhaps this is why Jesus invites us all to become like little children.

St. Paul reminds us in Romans 8:6–11 that the same spirit that raised Jesus Christ of Nazareth from the dead lives within us.

WHAAAAT?

Yes, that's right, we live and move and have our being as believers in Christ with the spirit of Christ living within us. We live Within the Omnipresent Wonder of Christ: W.O.W.

Saint Mother Teresa used the analogy of a fish in water.

Where ever we swim during this journey of life we are engulfed by the love of God, the spirit of Christ is behind us, before us, beneath us, above us, within us urging us to think like Jesus, understand others like Jesus, forgive like Jesus, and lighten up and live like Jesus who, as we are told in scripture, was not confined by status or the opinions of other people. When you are made new in Christ, the old way of thinking is gone and the new thinking in Christ is resurrected. Your mind is governed by the Spirit which results in life and peace.

I grew up in Long Island, NY and during my B.C. days (before Christ became the Lord of my life) I used to drop the "F" word like a ghetto gangster as my mind was certainly controlled by my flesh. I remember one time a close friend called me out on my language, but I brushed him off with another curse word.

After Jesus took up residence within my interior castle I had absolutely no desire to use that word again. My mouth was the first zone of interior cleaning that was resurrected into the likeness of Christ. The result? A light, kind and compassionate shift in my intonation and word choice. Jesus is always recovering the lighter version of who we are created to be.

When your mind is controlled by the flesh, your identity is hijacked and confusion, suspicion, doubt, and worry slither in between your two ears and spill out into your perceptions and behaviors.

## Refresh Your Identity in Christ:

Identify the thoughts you will often entertain that are governed (controlled, influenced, or regulated) by the flesh (worldly desires, selfish ambitions and vain conceits)?

When you bring the light of your presence on the thoughts that fuel death to your inner peace, joy, and confidence in the Lord, you are now in a position to SHIFT them into the light of Christ's presence within you and transfer that awareness into a positive behavior.

For example: At times I will have a critical thought after facilitating a training that questions if the training was good enough and suggests that I should have done more. This thought robs me of inner peace and confidence because it is fueled by a worldly desire to be enough.

How do I know? Because this thought is never satisfied, the more I feed it with my efforts and attention, the more it wants. It's never enough.

Once I became aware of my mind being governed by the flesh before and after an event, I began implementing the behavior of prayer.

*Dear Lord, thank You for the opportunity to facilitate growth and learning in the lives of people entrusted to my care. I invite You to remind me that this is your work through me. Bless the words of my mouth and the meditations of my heart that You would be glorified in all of my efforts. More of You, less of me. Grant me the peace of knowing that with You living in and through me, all things are possible.*

*"With man this is impossible, but with God all things are possible."* John 19:26

When you have a thought that robs your inner peace and confident identity in Christ, explore its source: the flesh is never satisfied, it always wants more and is fueled by insecurity, criticism, suspicion, fear, doubt, and worry.

The Spirit is always willing to learn, grow, adjust, forgive, release, and begin again with confidence and trust in God resulting in peace and life.

Many times, simply the conscious choice to die to yourself—your own desires—requires that you consider the needs of others above your own. This will SHIFT the governing of your mind from the flesh to the spirit.

Do you desire to be understood? Then make it your daily practice to understand other people's perspectives and life experiences. Jesus created instant connections with people because he loved first and then offered guidance.

Do you desire to experience more open doors in your life? Then make it your practice to create open doors for those around you.

Do you desire to experience generosity from other people? Then make it your practice to be generous with your time and talents to people around you.

Do you desire to experience more loving moments that are filled with laughter and joy? Then create loving moments, laugh more, and play with those around you.

Live each moment this week within the W.O.W. You have the same spirit that raised Jesus from the grave. Invite the Spirit of

Christ to govern your mind and life and peace will become your way in all things.

> *Lord, when my mind is controlled by your spirit, I feel that all things are possible, I remember who I am and what I am not. My peace is expanded, and my life feels more complete as I surrender all to You. I invite You today to rock my interior world with the power of your spirit within me. Take charge of my mind, will, and emotions so much that when people see me they walk away with a sense of how much You love and adore them. My greatest joy comes in the measure through which I love and serve others. My ego is too big to make that happen on my own, so crash my pity parties and self-oriented thinking that is fueled by the fleshly desires to be seen, acknowledged, and recognized. Help me to feel safe and connected being small in You with full confidence that when I am controlled by your presence within me then my true identity is found, my peace is profound, and my life is secure. Keep me W.O.W.'d this week: Within your Omnipresent Wonder.*

*L.O.V.E. Learning Circle: Clarity of Focus Leads to Accuracy of Response:*

L: **LEARN & LISTEN:** What's in this verse or phrase, tip or technique that will help me anchor my identity in Christ more today than yesterday?

_____

_____

_____

_____

O: **OBSERVE:** My 1–3 gold nuggets I want to remember and pull into behavior:

_____

_____

_____

V: **VISUALIZE:** Visualize integrating the meaningful verses and messages into your daily life. What will you notice to be different in your thoughts, perceptions and behaviors?

_____

_____

_____

_____

E: **EXPLORE:** Explore one specific forward action step you commit to taking in the coming days to help anchor your identity in Christ. Explore what you will notice to be different personally and professionally as you apply today's learnings.

_____

_____

_____

_____

# RE-BOOT YOUR IDENTITY WITH ONE QUESTION

*"Come to me, all you who are weary and burdened, and I will give you rest"* (Matthew 11:28).

S implicity: *the quality or condition of being easy to understand or do.*

What if as your next day rolls in you sift your thoughts through the filter of simplicity in Christ. Jesus was constantly going for healing and restoration.

Explore one question as you jump into your week:

How can I be a more relaxed and simplified version of me in Christ?

When your sense of self (your identity) spills out of you into the world around you, tension increases and your body reacts with stress and anxiety.

What if you took this one question along with you every day, how would you imagine this practice might open up opportunities to "do life" with less stress? Remember, stress is the power you give to outside circumstance to define what you believe you are capable of handling successfully.

This is a question that came to me when I found myself in a fetal position, lying exhausted in bed, after half a year of chemo treatments and nine surgeries as I made my way through advanced cancer back to complete restoration, at this point in the journey, I was half way through.

The question: how can I be a more relaxed version of me in Christ, followed a proclamation I made during the same time period: *"WOW I never realized how much energy it takes to be me."* In fact, it took so much energy to be me that it almost killed me.

Energy is your capacity for action. It shows up in the form of positive or negative behavior.

When Jesus sits on the throne of your mind, will, and emotions you tap into an endless supply of energy.

When your mind, will, and emotions are controlled by the world and self-interest you will rise and fall in your capacity for action depending upon how the world judges you at that moment in time.

I can honestly say that as the Lord carried me through a divorce, double mastectomy, 16 chemos, a year of additional chemotherapy treatments, six weeks of daily radiation, 14 surgeries (due to 3rd degree burns on my chest from the chemo/radiation combination they had to graft my back onto my front . . . as I often mention I don't know if I am coming or going most days, a sense of humor diffuses stress), a MRSA staph infection and additional experimental treatments, I was NEVER left empty handed in the present moment when it came to the grace, strength, and peace I needed to move through the next step in my healing journey. God is the great "I AM" who shows up NOW: I can do all things through Christ who gives me strength . . . not just a few things . . . ALL things through Christ (Philippians 4:13).

*Don't wait to give yourself permission to slow down, become a more relaxed version of you in Christ and smell the roses until your body is screaming so loudly you are literally taken out of the game of life.*

Living in simplicity involves the ability to tune into the one thing of highest importance in the moment along with the energy to carry it out, utilizing the gift of the spirit: self-control to minimize futile distractions.

Simplicity requires high noticing around your schedule and allows itself to be interrupted for those moments that align with what you value most while avoiding behavior that sucks the energy right out of you: gossip, social media, mind-reading.

Simplicity in Christ gives more authority to the strength of God within you than the circumstance outside of you and looks at situations with curiosity and fascination, trusting that God is always working out everything for an ultimate good for those who love and trust in Him.

Simplicity is unattached to shiny objects that have no lasting value and anchors itself in what is good, right, true, beautiful, excellent and praiseworthy in and through Christ. Similar to the young child that Jesus used as an example to the disciples to share a lesson on humility, simplicity does not know how to be one way and act another.

Your true identity in Christ lives in the space of simplicity just as Jesus declared the two greatest commandments:

- Love the Lord your God with all your heart, mind, soul, and strength.
- Love your neighbor as yourself.

Not rocket science, right? Yet it requires an intentional choice on your part to be a more relaxed version of you in Christ.

## Refresh Your Identity in Christ:

Step off the stage of drama quicker today than yesterday; forgive quicker today than yesterday; release negative thinking including judgements towards self and others quicker today than yesterday; choose a kind, gentle intonation, facial expression, and body language that reflects a more relaxed version of you in Christ today.

Explore a few of the questions below and pull out one or two that resonate with you.

Take 15 minutes and journal your response and pin it up by your workspace as a reminder to slow down and practice being a more relaxed version of you in Christ:

- *What can I shift in my intonation that would reflect a more relaxed version of me in Christ (make Jesus recognizable) in conversions I have with my loved ones? Colleagues?*
- *How can I shift my body language to reflect a more relaxed version of me in Christ?*
- *How can I be more relaxed preparing for a work project?*
- *What can I shift today to make room for interruptions that God prompts (divine appointments)?*
- *How can I give this presentation more relaxed in Christ?*
- *What if I brought a more relaxed version of me in Christ to the table as I explored solutions to my perceived conflict? What would that look like? Feel like? Sound like?*
- *What if I woke up tomorrow and I was a more relaxed version of me in Christ? What would I notice to be different? What value would I bring into the world as a result of a more relaxed version of me? How would this affect the relationships I care about?*
- *Would being a more relaxed version of me in Christ boost my confidence? How so?*

*Dear Lord, I give You permission to override me when I am living in the fast lane of life. Help me to be a more relaxed version of me as I surrender all I am to You with trust and confidence that Your yoke is easy and your burden is light. Fill me with your peace that You offer me in this present moment that guards my mind, will, and emotions from being troubled or afraid. Help me to rest in You as I explore a simplified, relaxed version of me in and through You. I'm excited to see what that will look like. I don't want to be one way and act another. Resurrect a childlike faith that has its identity anchored in You. Show me how to be the person You have created me to be: fearless and more relaxed in You. Make simplicity a daily experience. Less is more. Empower me with the ability to prune away those behaviors and projects that do not produce good fruit and create heaviness in my daily life and the lives of those entrusted to my care.*

*L.O.V.E. Learning Circle: Clarity of Focus Leads to Accuracy of Response:*

L: **LEARN & LISTEN:** What's in this verse or phrase, tip or technique that will help me anchor my identity in Christ more today than yesterday?

_____

_____

_____

_____

O: **OBSERVE:** My 1–3 gold nuggets I want to remember and pull into behavior:

_____

_____

_____

_____

V: **VISUALIZE:** Visualize integrating the meaningful verses and messages into your daily life. What will you notice to be different in your thoughts, perceptions and behaviors?

_____

_____

_____

_____

E: **EXPLORE:** Explore one specific forward action step you commit to taking in the coming days to help anchor your identity in Christ. Explore what you will notice to be different personally and professionally as you apply today's learnings.

_____

_____

_____

_____

# ABRACADABRA!

*"Do not conform to the pattern of this world, but be transformed by the renewing of your mind"* (Romans 12:2a).

*"We all stumble in many ways. Those who are never at fault in what they say are perfect, able to keep their whole body in check.*

*"When we put bits into the mouths of horses to make them obey us, we can turn the whole animal. Or take ships as an example. Although they are so large and are driven by strong winds, they are steered by a very small rudder wherever the pilot wants to go. Likewise, the tongue is a small part of the body, but it makes great boasts. Consider what a great forest is set on fire by a small spark. The tongue also is a fire, a world of evil among the parts of the body. It corrupts the whole person, sets the whole course of one's life on fire, and is itself set on fire by hell. All kinds of animals, birds, reptiles, and sea creatures are being tamed and have been tamed by human beings, but no one can tame the tongue. It is a restless evil, full of deadly poison.*

*"With the tongue we praise our Lord and Father, and with it we curse human beings, who have been made in God's likeness. Out of the same mouth come praise and cursing. My brothers and sisters, this should not be. Can both fresh water and*

*saltwater flow from the same spring? My brothers and sisters, can a fig tree bear olives, or a grapevine bear figs? Neither can a salt spring produce fresh water"* (James 3:2-12).

Did you ever play make-believe as a child and use the word Abracadabra? It is actually an ancient Aramaic statement which is the practice of thinking and speaking positive thoughts which create and imprint a positive speech habit (*SHIFT Leadership Training*).

The Bible references the power of the tongue and its ability to set the life of man on fire. The fire can be fueled by the Holy Spirit for God's glory or it can destroy your life and those around you, depending upon the words you use. The good news is that you get to choose your words every day.

Today pay close attention to your inner voice: the words and phrases you choose to dwell on. Whatever you focus on grows BIGGER. If you want a lighter version of you then don't let your words be your BOSS.Be the boss of the words you use to describe your life experience as well as what you believe about your ability to overcome versus being overcome by circumstances.

Speak LIFE into your inner thoughts. Give more authority to the strength of God within you than to your worldly circumstances.

Observe and delete any of the following negative choice points and replace them with life- giving words: kind, loving and supportive speech to yourself and others . . . invite the Holy Spirit to help you clean out your mind.

Avoid negative word choices that shut down or restrict your life and result in a heavier version of you (mentally speaking).:

**UNIVERSAL QUANTIFIERS:** Always, Never, No one, Nothing, Nobody, Everybody, Everything: these words create all or nothing thinking and will prevent the brain from tuning into a variety of available options needing for solution -based thinking.

**MODAL OPERATORS OF NECESSITY:** Have to, I need to, I should, I must, I can't . . . it's necessary: this type of thinking and speaking indicates a lack of choice and keep you stuck in mental muck.

As you expand your ability to explore and tune into several different options you will ignite solution-based thinking.

Words to use that benefit you are: expand, explore, consider, trust, look into, ignite, curious, enjoy, fascinating, and tell me more.

Let's explore pulling simplicity into your life this week and creating a lighter version of you. I invite you for the next week to take a negative thought FAST. Negative interior scripts lead to exterior drama, heaviness, and stress.

Explore fasting from the following *Lights Off* behavior shift below. In SHIFT Leadership Training we use the phrase: *Lights On* and *Lights Off,* to describe specific behavior that expands positive energy (Lights On) or retracts it (Lights Off). Energy is your capacity for action.

For example, "trust" is considered a *Lights On* response to life and is solution focused (boosts your energy). "Fear" is considered a *Lights Off* reactive response to life and is problem focused (drains your energy). Below are a few behaviors that result from "Lights Off" thinking patterns.

What do you think would SHIFT in your perspectives this week and your capacity for action if you intentionally fasted from negative thoughts which are often manifested in the following two behaviors?

**Blaming**
Any time you blame yourself or another person take a step back from the situation and ask yourself what are you refusing to take responsibility for . . . it may come down to taking responsibility for your own sense of inner peace, joy, and happiness.

**Complaining**
Complaining of any kind creates an exchange of negative energy between you and yourself OR between you and another person, resulting in shrinking your brain and blocking your ability to tune into available resources. Think about the last time you complained

about something to someone or someone complained to you. Did you feel drained or energized after the experience?

Common thoughts that usually fuel the above behaviors are: nothing ever works out for me; I never get an opportunity to shine; nobody ever listens to me. These words flow from identity theft. Did you forget you do not belong to the world? Do not touch, do not taste. Christ died and rose again to win you over to life.

## Refresh Your Identity in Christ:

Prune for growth the negative, heavy scripts you have been using and write a script that reflects simplicity and a lighter version of you in Christ as discussed in the lesson: *Reboot Your Identity with One Question.*

Erase one negative thought at a time and replace it with a positive thought. For example:

- **Erase:** *"I am feeling some fear around giving this presentation to the board."*
- **Replace with:** *"I trust in the Lord with all my heart that I have the God given ability to present easily and naturally the information contained within the proposal to the board. I have successfully moved through challenging presentations before and I believe I will do it again. The Lord is my confidence, all things are possible."*

By your thoughts you form your words, by your words you form your conclusions, by your conclusions you form your perceptions and by your perceptions you give birth to your attitude.

Your attitude is your closest friend or worst enemy. Is life for you? (light and simple) or against you? (heavy and complex). The choice is yours and makes all the difference in the outcomes you experience.

*Dear Lord, help me to remember the power of my words to build up and edify or to tear down and destroy. Sift my inner self talk and erase the words that are fueling death and destruction in my life. One ugly word repeated over time has the power to burn down a forest that took years to grow. Wake me up to the connection between my identity in You and the words I use towards myself and those around me. Help me to master my inner self talk and erase those familiar statements that suck the life right out of me. Replace the space they occupied with words that ignite healthy growth and life in You. You are the master landscaper of my mind. Make it a beautiful garden where it is safe to linger and refresh my soul. Pull out the weeds of negative self-talk and words that imprison me and those around me. I am willing this week to be bumped by You just before a destructive word is about to spill out of my mouth. Weed out all gossip and judging speech, all ugly talk and negative behavior that goes along with it. Just as Joseph ran from another man's wife so as to avoid sin, help me to cover my mouth and run into another room when I feel that a misplaced ugly word, usually fueled by my need to be right, liked, understood, seen, acknowledged, or recognized comes slithering out of my mouth. I want to speak life into each moment and carry life through my words to those entrusted to my care.*

*L.O.V.E. Learning Circle: Clarity of Focus Leads to Accuracy of Response:*

L: **LEARN & LISTEN:** What's in this verse or phrase, tip or technique that will help me anchor my identity in Christ more today than yesterday?

_____

_____

_____

_____

O: **OBSERVE:** My 1–3 gold nuggets I want to remember and pull into behavior:

_____

_____

_____

_____

V: **VISUALIZE:** Visualize integrating the meaningful verses and messages into your daily life. What will you notice to be different in your thoughts, perceptions, and behaviors?

_____

_____

_____

_____

E: **EXPLORE:** Explore one specific forward action step you commit to taking in the coming days to help anchor your identity in Christ. Explore what you will notice to be different personally and professionally as you apply today's learnings.

_____

_____

_____

_____

# YOU KNOW WHAT YOU NEED TO KNOW

"Moses said to the LORD, 'Pardon your servant, Lord. I have never been eloquent, neither in the past nor since You have spoken to your servant. I am slow of speech and of tongue.'

"Then the LORD said to him, 'Who gave human beings their mouths? Who makes them deaf or mute? Who gives them sight or makes them blind? Is it not I, the LORD? Now go; I will help you speak and will teach you what to say.'

"But Moses said, 'Pardon your servant, Lord. Please send someone else' " (Exodus 4:10–13).

How many times have you questioned your ability?

When you question your ability, you question the Creator who equipped you and still equips you with your ability through Him. Think about that. The Creator of this universe knit you together in your mother's womb and has equipped you with strengths, talents, and spiritual gifts.

When you rely on and use your God-given strengths, talents, and spiritual gifts you are doing what you were placed here on earth to do: Bring glory and honor to God! That is our purpose here on earth and where we should park our identity.

Is your identity deeply rooted in praising, honoring, and bringing God glory?

I know for myself personally, I need refreshment in this area. I put way too much trust in myself and my abilities rather than placing my trust solely in God.

We can see this illustrated throughout the Bible. Moses questions his ability to speak. Moses is thinking with his "lights off" and not with his "lights on". Moses is responding out of fear and focusing on how he views himself and not focusing on how God views him, and the power God will provide when he begins to speak.

Moses exhibits a lack of faith. He is not trusting God. God responds: *"Who has made man's mouth? Who makes him mute, or deaf, or seeing, or blind? Is it not I, the LORD?'*

We need to remember that God has the power to work in and through that which He has created. Read that sentence again.

Do you believe that God has the power to work in and through which He has created?

That means that God can work through you.

We need to step aside and park our Ego and pride to allow God to show up to do the work He has created us to do. We are just instruments of God carrying out His plan.

Are you willing to show up and faithfully listen to God or will you rely on your own strength and run away?

Do you believe that God will show up and give you what you need in the moment?

In the New Testament, Jesus was preparing his disciples for his departure. He had been "doing life" with his disciples for approximately three years. Jesus knew His time on earth was limited and wanted to assure His disciples that even though he had been walking side by side with them that he would need to depart to fulfill something even greater.

*"But very truly I tell you, it is for your good that I am going away. Unless I go away, the Advocate will not come to you; but if I go, I will send Him to you"* (John 16:7).

The Advocate is the Holy Spirit. As Christians if we believe in Jesus Christ and surrender our lives to Him, we are given this same Advocate. We have the same Spirit that raised Jesus Christ from the grave living within us. (Romans 8:11)

AMAZING! Let's break this down. The Holy Spirit that resides in us after our surrender to Christ is the same Spirit that raised Jesus from the dead. If that doesn't evoke confidence and courage, I am not sure what will. Acknowledging this daily can be transformative and empowering in our daily walk.

When life happens and you are paralyzed by fear, remember that you've got the power through Jesus Christ.

*"When you are brought before synagogues, rulers, and authorities, do not worry about how you will defend yourselves or what you will say, for the Holy Spirit will teach you at that time what you should say"* (Luke 12: 11–12).

Don't worry about defending your faith when you come up to people to talk. Don't think, "I don't know enough about the Bible, God, or Jesus". This passage says, "Don't worry when you go up in front of them because the Holy Spirit will teach you ***at that time*** what you should say".

It doesn't say he's going to tell you ahead of time what to say, and that's the annoying part for most of us. We want to be prepared and have the exact words. This is where faith is required to rely on the Holy Spirit.

The Spirit of God lives in you. That means that any time you are called to defend your faith, say something, or speak up about God, the Holy Spirit will intercede on your behalf if you are willing to trust and surrender.

Knowing this is so important because most often we don't speak up because of fear.

We fear that we don't know enough. When this happens, we are relying on ourselves and we don't really believe that God's going to give us the right words to say.

In obedience to God, He will give you the words to say! It's not about us and our intellect, and us always knowing more, but there's something spiritual that takes place. Do you believe that something supernatural will happen in your life when you just speak up and start talking about God?

At the sunset of this life it will come down to a simple question: "Who did I positively impact for Christ?" I can think of times when I was scared, became intimidated, and just kept my mouth shut. I worried about what others were going to say or think about me.

Remember, when you put your trust in the Lord and rely on the Holy Spirit to give you the words, you will know "what you need to know" and that is liberating. Your identity in Christ fuels trust and confidence.

## Refresh Your Identity in Christ:

This week take time to notice when fear creeps in and begins to steal your voice. Remember God will place opportunities right in front of you this week to speak up in order to bring Him praise, glory, and honor. The Holy Spirit will give you the exact words to say.

Observe this week when God presents you with an opportunity to trust Him with your words and speech. Did you walk through the door God opened and speak up by relying on Him, or did you fail to walk through the door of opportunity?

Use the chart below to record the situation, reaction, and notes of your learning.

| Spoke Up / Or Failed to Speak Up in Your Own Flesh | Spoke Up by the Power of the Holy Spirit |
|---|---|
| Monday:<br><br>Situation—<br><br>Reaction—<br><br>Notes— | Monday:<br><br>Situation—<br><br>Reaction—<br><br>Notes— |
| Tuesday:<br><br>Situation—<br><br>Reaction—<br><br>Notes— | Tuesday:<br><br>Situation—<br><br>Reaction—<br><br>Notes— |
| Wednesday:<br><br>Situation—<br><br>Reaction—<br><br>Notes— | Wednesday:<br><br>Situation—<br><br>Reaction—<br><br>Notes— |
| Thursday:<br><br>Situation—<br><br>Reaction—<br><br>Notes— | Thursday:<br><br>Situation—<br><br>Reaction—<br><br>Notes— |
| Friday:<br><br>Situation—<br><br>Reaction—<br><br>Notes— | Friday:<br><br>Situation—<br><br>Reaction—<br><br>Notes— |
| Saturday:<br><br>Situation—<br><br>Reaction—<br><br>Notes— | Saturday:<br><br>Situation—<br><br>Reaction—<br><br>Notes— |

| Spoke Up / Or Failed to Speak Up in Your Own Flesh | Spoke Up by the Power of the Holy Spirit |
|---|---|
| Sunday: | Sunday: |
| Situation— | Situation— |
| Reaction— | Reaction— |
| Notes— | Notes— |

*Dear God, I can't even begin to count the times that I failed to speak on Your behalf because I got in my own way. Please help me to get out of the way so that I can be used by You daily, relying on You to be the exact portion that I need for that day. Nothing more, nothing less. When faced with other people's perception of my identity, please give me the strength to walk through the door that You have opened and equip me with the exact words to say for that moment. Let me experience boldness, confidence, and courage to open my mouth in all the moments that are set before me to bring You praise, glory, and honor. When I fail to rely on your strength for Your words and shrink back in fear, give me grace and provide me with additional opportunities to be used for Your Kingdom. I love You Lord God and I know that I am nothing without You! Amen.*

*L.O.V.E. Learning Circle: Clarity of Focus Leads to Accuracy of Response:*

L: **LEARN & LISTEN:** What's in this verse or phrase, tip or technique that will help me anchor my identity in Christ more today than yesterday?

_____

_____

_____

_____

O: **OBSERVE:** My 1–3 gold nuggets I want to remember and pull into behavior:

_____

_____

_____

_____

V: **VISUALIZE:** Visualize integrating the meaningful verses and messages into your daily life. What will you notice to be different in your thoughts, perceptions, and behaviors?

_____

_____

_____

_____

E: **EXPLORE:** Explore one specific forward action step you commit to taking in the coming days to help anchor your identity in Christ. Explore what you will notice to be different personally and professionally as you apply today's learnings.

_____

_____

_____

_____

# Fallen, Not Forgotten

*"All this I have told you so that you will not fall away"*
(John 16:1).

When I first started to explore the meaning of this passage, I focused my mind on the words "fall away" and asked myself, "Falling away from what?" What does Jesus know about my behavior that I am not yet aware of? What will I be falling away from? Every word that Jesus spoke is worth examining and applicable to our lives today.

Jesus knows that we will be distracted by the bright shiny objects that might lead to our stumbling, falling away, and back sliding.

Our identity in Christ can be hindered and we can fall, stumble, and back slide when we elevate popularity, possessions, people, position and pace above placing our identity in Christ.

Jesus knew that his disciples would fall away, and He knows that we will too at times.

Jesus had been preparing His disciples and giving them glimpses into what was to come.

Let's look at Peter. Peter is both hope and heartache wrapped into one. I like to say that Peter over promises and under delivers throughout his ministry, however, Jesus is always by his side and Peter always comes back after momentary lapses.

Jesus asked His disciples, "Who do people say the Son of Man is?"

> " 'But what about you?' he asked. 'Who do you say I am?'
>
> "Simon Peter answered, 'You are the Messiah, the Son of the living God.'
>
> "Jesus replied, 'Blessed are you, Simon son of Jonah, for this was not revealed to you by flesh and blood, but by My Father in heaven. And I tell you that you are Peter, and on this rock, I will build My church, and the gates of death will not overcome it. I will give you the keys of the kingdom of heaven; whatever you bind on earth will be bound in heaven, and whatever you loose on earth will be loosed in heaven.' " (Matthew 16: 15–19).

Peter proclaimed that Jesus was the Messiah, the Son of the living God.

Right after proclaiming that Jesus was the Messiah, Peter rebuked Jesus.

> "Peter took Him aside and began to rebuke Him. 'Never, Lord!' he said. 'This shall never happen to You!'
>
> "Jesus turned and said to Peter, 'Get behind me, Satan! You are a stumbling block to Me; you do not have in mind the concerns of God, but merely human concerns' " (Matthew 16:22–23).

Peter was getting distracted by the temporal shiny objects of that time. He was putting more emphasis on his plan than on Jesus' eternal plan. Peter's momentary lapse was attributed to Peter rebuking the Lord immediately after Jesus had declared that, on this rock (Peter) I will build my church.

Like Peter, we suffer with human limitations that are wrapped up in our identity.

Peter has an opportunity again to identify himself as a follower of Christ and once again, he falls and fails in his response.

By taking his eyes off Jesus, Peter temporarily fell away from the Lord. His identity was overcome by Satan.

This wouldn't be the last time that Peter would turn his back on Jesus.

Peter is also famously known for denying Jesus. Jesus even predicts that Peter will deny Him.

> " 'Simon, Simon, Satan has asked to sift all of you as wheat.
> But I have prayed for you, Simon, that your faith may not fail.
> And when you have turned back, strengthen your brothers.'
>
> "But he replied, 'Lord, I am ready to go with You both to prison
> and to death' " (Luke 22:31–33).

Peter is hopeful now that he is ready to go with Jesus to both prison and death, however shortly after proclaiming this, Peter denies Jesus three times.

"Then seizing Him, they led Him away and took Him into the house of the high priest.

Peter followed at a distance. And when some there had kindled a fire in the middle of the courtyard and had sat down together, Peter sat down among them. A servant girl saw him seated there in the firelight. She looked closely at him and said, '*This man was with him.*'

> "But he denied it. 'Woman, I do not know him,' he said" (Luke
> 22:54-57).

In a couple of short verses, Peter had fallen once again and denied Jesus even after proclaiming that he would go to both prison and death for Jesus.

Peter breaks both promises. He denies Jesus and he lets other people's perceptions identify him. He farms out his position as a follower of Christ to other people's perceptions. He sold himself out.

How many times do we compromise or sell ourselves out to the cost of perception?

Thankfully for Peter the story does not end here. Even though Peter falls away at times, he is never forgotten by God.

Jesus, out of grace, restores Peter's position over the flock. Jesus did not leave Peter when Peter fell away. Peter left, not Jesus. Jesus did not forget Peter, even when he fell.

*"When they had finished eating, Jesus said to Simon Peter,
'Simon son of John, do you love Me more than these?'*

*" 'Yes, Lord,' he said, 'You know that I love You.'*

*"Jesus said, 'Feed my lambs.'*

*"Again, Jesus said, 'Simon son of John, do you love me?'*

*"He answered, 'Yes, Lord, You know that I love You.'*

*"Jesus said, 'Take care of my sheep.'*

*"The third time he said to him, 'Simon son of John, do
you love me?'*

*"Peter was hurt because Jesus asked him the third time, 'Do
you love me?' He said, 'Lord, You know all things; You know
that I love You.'*

*"Jesus said, 'Feed my sheep. Very truly I tell you, when you were
younger you dressed yourself and went where you wanted; but
when you are old you will stretch out your hands, and someone
else will dress you and lead you where you do not want to go.'
Jesus said this to indicate the kind of death by which Peter
would glorify God. Then he said to him, 'Follow me!' "* (John
21:15–19).

Jesus reinstates Peter's position.

Reinstate is defined as: "restore (someone or something) to their
former position or condition."

Jesus has the transformative power to reinstate our identity in Him.
He can restore you to your former position. That is GREAT news!

## Refresh Your Identity in Christ:

Take stock of your current reality. Have you fallen away from your
position in Christ? Are there areas that you need to hand over and
give to God in order to be reinstated?

Remember, Jesus says you will fall away. This is our human nature,
this is sin. However, when we fall away, we will not be forgotten,

and the almighty God has a way of bringing us back even though we don't deserve it. God is just, merciful, and full of grace.

Write these three truths and place them visibly in front of you this week.

- Jesus is faithful.
- He is calling us to be faithful.
- We remain faithful by remembering His works and His words.

*Dear God, as I enter this day please remind me where I might have fallen away from Your commands, Your plan, and Your purpose for my life. Please forgive me for my sin in my fall. I know that I am undeserving of Your grace. You paid the ultimate price on the cross for my sins. My falling away hammered the nails into Your flesh. My sin and the sin of all the world You took to the cross. Even though I fall away, You never forget us and continue to pursue us even though we don't deserve it. Please shine a piercing light into the deepest parts of my soul to reveal to me the areas I need to turn over to You ; areas where I have fallen away, areas that only You can reinstate. I love You Lord with all my strength, with all my heart, and all of my soul in my limited human capacity.*

*L.O.V.E. Learning Circle: Clarity of Focus Leads to Accuracy of Response:*

L: **LEARN & LISTEN:** What's in this verse or phrase, tip or technique that will help me anchor my identity in Christ more today than yesterday?

_____

_____

_____

_____

O: **OBSERVE:** My 1–3 gold nuggets I want to remember and pull into behavior:

_____

_____

_____

_____

V: **VISUALIZE:** Visualize integrating the meaningful verses and messages into your daily life. What will you notice to be different in your thoughts, perceptions and behaviors?

_____

_____

_____

_____

E: **EXPLORE:** Explore one specific forward action step you commit to taking in the coming days to help anchor your identity in Christ. Explore what you will notice to be different personally and professionally as you apply today's learnings.

_____

_____

_____

_____

# A THREE STEP
# PRISON BREAK

Jesus was the ultimate ERR doctor as you will see as we reflect on the lives of five people who were imprisoned by their life style and/or doubt which resulted in identity theft: Peter, Mary, Zacchaeus, Thomas, and Paul and the FREEDOM they gained as a result of an Encounter (E) with Jesus which led to Repentance (R) and a Resurrection (R) of purpose and identity, they experienced a break out of the cocoon of worldly restrictions and embraced The One who died to give them the ability to soar.

The caterpillar has the DNA of a butterfly, yet the predators of the world too often snatch it up before it transforms and embraces its ability to fly.

You have the DNA of God as you are created in the image and likeness of God. You have the ability to soar through the storms of life. All things are possible for you when it comes to mastering your mind for transformation and revival. Jesus meets you and escorts you back into revival as you break down the interior damns that hold back the streams of life-giving living water flowing within you.

Too often you play small: lacking fuel and scarcity thinking. Similar to Thomas's doubt that blocked his ability to trust and believe: you are often blinded by the trickery of smoke and mirrors that Satan uses to distract you from the way out of your slavery to fear, doubt, and worry.

Similar to Peter's outbursts of anger and frustration: you will get spun into the cocoon of EGO, edging God out of your perspectives, conclusions, and plans and forgetting that The One who calls you is faithful. He will provide a way out as He did for Peter when He filled his empty net with fish. Jesus moved beyond Peter's frustration to the ultimate goal: to set him free from the restriction of his desires and unmet needs so that he could fly.

Anger often rears its ugly head in the behavior of stonewalling, defensive behavior, and unkind words (towards others and yourself). Frustration is fueled by the need to be right, liked, and understood and chains you in the prison of the shadow side of your positionality and false beliefs. Have you had enough?

What predators are threatening your ability to fly in Christ's strength and God's will for you in life?

Imagine a triangle and at the top of the triangle you have your Will. The left corner of the triangle represents your Mind and the right corner of the triangle represents your Emotions.

Your Will directly influences your Mind (your, thoughts, perceptions, conclusions, assumptions, beliefs) which directly impacts your emotions (what you feel: sad, happy, angry, frustrated, all of which create your attitude.

An emotion is your body's response to your thought life. Your attitude is your closest friend or worst enemy and you get to choose it. How? By surrendering it up to God for His will to be done in and through your life (Edging God In) OR not.

God has given us free will and you can choose to sit yourself on the throne of your Will as was the case in the Garden of Eden: deception, confusion, accusation and self-doubt all play in the space of a Will directed by self (Edging God Out). **Will => Mind => Emotions => Attitude.**

Five prominent players from the New Testament were all trapped in the cocoon of worldly strongholds: hunger for power, popularity, passion and position: Peter, Zacchaeus, Mary Magdalene, Thomas, and Paul. They forgot they had wings to fly.

Jesus being the prison freeing, chain breaking, cocoon freeing Savior meets them all in their restricted state of being and set them free. Once they encounter the humble love of Christ, they relinquish control over their own Wills and receive the key that sets then free: Surrendering their Wills over to God's Will. (Read Galatians 2:2.)

Let's take a closer look at five people from the New Testament whose personal encounter with the Lord resulted in a resurrected identity and purpose:

1. **Peter: Luke 5:1-11:** Peter's encounter with Jesus: Peter is a self-motivated entrepreneur who is dedicated to revenue producing behavior; however, when his labor does not produce the desired outcome, he is left wallowing in a cocoon of self-pity, victimization, and frustration. Can you relate? When was a time when you cast your net out into the world only to pull in an empty net? Jesus ignored Peter's victimization and pity party and invited him to jump back in his boat.

   The difference this time as Peter cast his net, is monumental: rather than by his own will and sheer determination to produce a desired outcome, Peter was now accompanied by the King of Kings and Lord of Lords. *Jesus was in the "BOAT" and initiated the catch and the outcome was more than Peter could have imagined."*

   *Reflect upon a time in your life when you came out of a situation after giving it YOUR all, exhausted and defeated and you encountered Jesus. What was the outcome as a result of your encounter with Jesus? How did you repent from self-focus (I centered Will)? What did you resurrect? For example, Peter resurrected a faith-filled attitude of trust as he laid his will down and surrendered to Jesus as he proclaimed, "Get away from me LORD for I am a sinful man!"*

Peter's encounter with Jesus resulted in repentance from self-focused efforts that had their foundation on ego: *I want this outcome for my own advancement, and I didn't get what I wanted so I am imprisoned in the cocoon of frustration.*

2. **Zacchaeus: Luke 19: 1-9:** Zacchaeus's encounter with Jesus: Zacchaeus had gumption (a shrewd or spirited initiative and resourcefulness). He wanted to see Jesus and knew he was too short in the midst of the crowds, so he climbed a tree.

As a result, Jesus recognized his gumption that overcame a physical limitation and entered into his life. He ate at his table, with his friends and won his heart over to repentance and a resurrected life.

Zacchaeus was stuck in the cocoon of worldly power and possessions that damaged his moral compass. The love and acceptance from Jesus (*the encounter*), in the midst of his sinful small and restricted negative behaviors resulted in a prison break and resurrected life. Zacchaeus regained his ability to fly.

Reflect on the following excerpt taken from *Hearing His Whisper . . . With Every Storm Jesus Comes Too*: Journal Entry: *May 20, 2001.* Notice that it was Zacchaeus's personal experience with the love of the Lord that resurrected and renewed his authentic identity in Christ and resulted in the behavior of generosity towards others:

*Me: I used to think that I knew the perfect way to get to you, Lord. I found myself judging others if they went another way. I am starting to see that every human being has something to teach me . . . each soul reveals new insight into You and me. Show me how to touch every soul with love.*

*Jesus: You cannot force yourself into the human heart. The hearts of my children are won over through unconditional love that is patiently poured out over time into their souls. To do this, you must first enter into their experiences . . . what moves their hearts, no matter how worldly it may seem to eyes that have been enlightened to heavenly things.*

*In order to win the confidence of a man's heart, you must first step into his world. Then you earn the right to speak the truth in love and he will listen because you have loved him where he is without judgment. Your love for him will increase within his heart the desire to do what is right in God's eyes.*

*Because God is love, he moves souls into his heart through love alone. Take Zacchaeus for example, one soul living in sin . . . I went to his house, ate his food at his table with his friends. I entered into his life experience with great love and acceptance. My love entering into his life exposed the dark deeds of his soul thereby leading him to repentance and reconciliation and a resurrected life purpose.*

*You must do the same to win hearts for me. It is pride and ego that keep you from stepping into the lives of those who are entranced by the things of the world . . . Do I not enter into your worldly experiences? Is it not my great love and mercy in spite of your acts of disobedience that continue to draw your heart into mine? Do the same for one another.*

*Love first, then lead. Follow my example . . . meet everyone on the road just as the father ran to meet the prodigal son. Go and meet others, love them, take time to listen, and experience their joys and sorrows . . . all with great love and mercy and in time you will earn the right to speak the truth in love. Through love and mercy their eyes will be opened to the condition of their soul . . . just as yours is.*

*Do not forget the depths from which you were saved so that pride will not draw you away from my love. It is the desire that I see . . . the desire always over the actions . . . offer the same grace to the souls around you . . . see others for who they desire to be . . . apart from all the pain that causes them to act out . . . just as I continue to see you.*

When have you encountered the love of the Lord that instantly resulted in positive behavior towards other people?

3. **Mary Magdalene: John 20: 11–18:** Mary Magdalene (most likely called Magdalene because she was from the town of Magdala, a fishing town on the coast of Galilee). Luke 8:2–3 speaks of seven demons that Jesus cast out of Mary which lead to her repentance and resurrected life following Jesus and traveling with Jesus and the twelve disciples from town to town.

   In John 20:11–18 Mary encounters the resurrected Jesus at the tomb and her faith is flipped from despair and sadness around death to joy and excitement around the resurrection.

   Because of her original encounter with Christ, through repentance of former ways of living that resulted from the possession by seven demons, Mary experienced a resurrected purpose and mission in life.

   Mary's identity went from being hijacked to being anchored in the lover of her soul.

   Mary followed Jesus to the grave. In spite of her personal experience of deliverance, Mary experienced doubt even in the presence of the Lord, as she pleaded with the Risen Lord thinking he is the gardener to show her where Jesus was taken. Interestingly, Mary's eyes were opened when Jesus called her name.

4. **Thomas: John 20:24-31:** Thomas is commonly known as "Doubting Thomas." In spite of the evidence and eyewitness accounts of the resurrected Lord, Thomas defends his positionality (ego), blocking his ability to believe. The result: no joy. His cocoon of doubt restricts his ability to grow wings and fly. Jesus crashed that party and offers the evidence Thomas declared, "Unless I put my hand in his side and my fingers in the holes of his hands I will not believe." What ultimatums have you declared over your life: "Unless I _____, I will not _____

_____." For example: Unless I achieve this specific status, I will not feel successful . . . or unless I get married, I will not feel complete.

Thomas's encounter is worth your reflection as it touches upon a shared human experience—doubt. Satan has been at this since the garden. "Did God really say that??" He is the ultimate spin doctor as he comes up with one-liners that twist your mind and compromise your emotions.

When your mind and emotions do not reflect the best version of you, explore the thoughts you have been focusing on. Doubt, suspicion, and taking offense easily are signs that your identity has been hijacked by the opinions or behaviors of other people.

Jesus' invitation to all of us began with his command to Thomas: "Stop doubting and BELIEVE." Give more authority to the strength of God's Holy Spirit within you than to your perceived circumstances, including the words and behavior of other people.

After Thomas encounters Jesus, he fell to his knees in repentance: "My Lord and my God." Jesus did not have to spend time edifying Thomas in the midst of his doubt and yet he did.

Jesus entered into Thomas's lack of faith and trust and pulled him in, through, and out of his doubt. The result was the resurrection of Thomas's conviction and faith.

Thomas represents our shared doubt and lack of faith. Perhaps we can learn from his repentance and join the blessed group that Jesus referenced: _Blessed are those who believe and do not need to see._

What are you resisting in your life that is flowing from your own self-doubt? Trust that God is good and has your best interests in mind? Belief that you are loved and adored by God? Worthy of God's forgiveness? Part of a bigger plan, orchestrated by the lover of your soul? What is it that is keeping you back from breaking out of your cocoon? Perhaps you have not yet encountered the humble, persistent love of Jesus? Invite Him in today.

5. **Paul, Saul of Tarsus: Acts 9:** Last but not least there is Paul, full of passion and conviction. Paul is the perfect example of a man who was imprisoned by his positionality. His cocoon of positionality was so tightly wound around his will that his moral compass was rocked. Killing Christians and destroying homes and families were just a few of the ramifications of his passion without Christ at the center of it.

   Paul's encounter with Christ offers us a crisp, clear witness of the transformation that can happen when the sinner meets the Savior, resulting in a 3-step prison break: An *Encounter* with Christ leads to *Repentance* and a *Resurrected* purpose and passion. It also led to a name change from Saul of Tarsus to Paul which represented his identity renewed in Christ.

   Filled with zeal, Paul was on the way to defend his positionality, as he was once again in route to kill more Christians and SHAZAM, Jesus jumps right between Paul's will and God's Will for Paul and knocks him to the ground.

   Perhaps it was the force of sin meeting the Savior . . . or the power of grafting a severed "shoot" (Paul) back into the Vine (Jesus). Either way the force from Paul's face to face encounter with Christ was enough to rock Paul's entire concept of who he was, why he was here, and why it mattered.

   Instantly Jesus began to retrieve Paul's lost identity and restore it back to its original positionality: *"You are a royal priesthood, a holy nation, a people belonging to God for the purpose of declaring His praises to the ends of the world."*

   Paul thrust his will into his positionality and lost his identity in the world. Jesus was determined to get it back. God is the hound from heaven and as the popular worship song by Cory

Asbury declares: No mountain you won't climb up, shadow you won't light up, coming after me . . . no wall you won't rip down, lie you won't tear down . . . coming after me.

## Refresh Your Identity in Christ:

Reflect on the following questions and explore times in your life that you failed to recognize the Risen Lord calling you back to your identity in Him. When have you exercised your free will in a way that imprisons your mind and negatively spins your emotions? **Encounter => Repentance => Resurrection**

When have you experienced an encounter with the Lord that resulted in repentance from negative behavior that compromised the person God is calling you to be? What were the ramifications of your choice to explore a change behavior that aligns with your identity in Christ?

What behavior still blocks your ability to expand your identity in Christ? For example, the need to be right blocks empathy and compassion.

Imagine and reflect for a moment what it was like for Mary to be freed from seven demons? What a thick cocoon of restriction she must have felt. The Lord saw her ability to fly and set her free from bondage. What has the Lord freed you from? Do you have specific hang-ups that keep your mind in the tomb of negative thinking, judgment, and fear? Take a moment to bind, rebuke, and cast out those hang-ups as you resurrect the mind of Christ and experience transformation by the renewing of your mind (Romans 12:2).

Similar to Thomas declaring doubt in his life, in what areas of your life are you imprisoned by doubt? What doubt are you declaring over your life? What specifically are you doubting? Where do you doubt? Who do you doubt? When do you doubt? What behavior occurs when you doubt? Thomas shut down in spite of being surrounded by joy from the good news: He has RISEN! Misery LOVES company. Gossip evokes gossip. Doubt evokes doubt. Are you harboring doubt in your cocoon and is it stunting the development of your wings which would allow you to experience a prison break and fly where God calls you to fly? (Jeremiah 29:11).

As a result of his encounter with Christ, Paul went on to be one of the most passionate and effective followers of Christ to this day. Jesus' gift of freedom is not confined by time or intensity.

Paul went from killing Christians to proclaiming Christ in a matter of days. Now that's a prison break worth reflecting upon.

Paul encountered Jesus, repented his sin, and entered into a resurrected life that was so radical and powerful that Jesus' followers felt fear when Paul knocked on their door after his conversion and jail break.

Paul also experienced a physical jail break when an angel of the Lord entered his prison cell, released the chains that bound him, and walked him out of the prison (Acts 5:19, Acts 12).

Are you sitting in a jail cell of your mind? Your own will? Your emotions?

Invite the Holy Spirit to do for you what the Angel did for Paul: remove your chains and walk you out of bondage. What would you imagine that would be like for you? What would you call your jail cell?

Here are a few examples: Self-pity; Judgment; Positionality that creates ugly behavior against those who do not share your positions; Fear of what people think; Doubt that God has your back and your best interests; Lack of trust; Lack of belief; Fear of failure. What is the name of your prison?

- Encounter Christ through intentional prayer and reflection on God's word throughout your day. Pick one of the five prominent players we explored and study them for a week. Reflect on their prison-breaks and how they relate to how you may feel trapped in your life today. Focus on their encounter with Christ and how it led to repentance and new lives.

- What do you want to pivot away from in your life that is blocking your ability to fly with Christ in this world?
- What do you want to expand in your life that would allow you to step out of your will and into God's will for you?
- Write a mission statement for your life with Christ that reflects your commitment to love the Lord with all of your heart, mind, soul, and strength and love your neighbor as yourself. Invite Jesus into the center of your will, mind, and emotions.
- An example mission statement: *I am committed to putting God's will above my own. I want what he wants, when he wants it, and how he wants it. I am here on God's time for His purpose so that He can make His appeal through me for the sake of the Salvation of Souls. Less of me and more of You, sweet Jesus, for your glory . . . not mine. My joy and peace are complete as I surrender all that I am into all that Jesus IS. Just Jesus.*

*Dear Lord, come and revive me. Wake up my perceptions and longings so that I have a singleness of heart around the desire to be loved and known by You. I can't give out to the world what I have not experienced within my own heart. Wake up Oh sleeper and rise from the dead and Christ will shine on you (Ephesians 5:13–14). Shine on me Lord, wake me up to want what You want me to have and pursue. I want a revival within my own life. Crash my party with Your irresistible presence and love! I want to encounter You more today than yesterday . . . to repent quicker today than yesterday, and to resurrect my identity in You more expansively today than yesterday. For without You I am nothing but with You I can hold up the weight of the world.*

*L.O.V.E. Learning Circle: Clarity of Focus Leads to Accuracy of Response:*

L: **LEARN & LISTEN:** What's in this verse or phrase, tip or technique that will help me anchor my identity in Christ more today than yesterday?

_____

_____

_____

O: **OBSERVE:** My 1–3 gold nuggets I want to remember and pull into behavior:

_____

_____

_____

_____

V: **VISUALIZE:** Visualize integrating the meaningful verses and messages into your daily life. What will you notice to be different in your thoughts, perceptions and behaviors?

_____

_____

_____

E: **EXPLORE:** Explore one specific forward action step you commit to taking in the coming days to help anchor your identity in Christ. Explore what you will notice to be different personally and professionally as you apply today's learnings.

_____

_____

_____

_____

# Six Logical Levels for Transformation

The following excerpt has been revised from *5 Minutes to Stress Relief* (by Lauren E Miller, Career Press/New Page Books, 2013 pp 107–113) and will give you a brief overview of a methodology taken from the field of neuro-linguistic programming (NLP) which is a system of alternative therapy intended to educate people in self-awareness and effective communication, and to model and change their patterns of mental and emotional behavior.

Throughout the experience of cancer and divorce, I participated in cognitive psychology therapy as well as energy psychology sessions. I was amazed at the powerful and quick transformations I experienced around deep emotional pain, using energy psychotherapy modalities such as Emotional Freedom Technique and NLP.

According to Susan Heitler, PhD, a clinical psychologist in Denver, *"Energy psychotherapies are to traditional psychotherapy as the alternative physical therapies like acupuncture are to medical treatment. We do not really know how or why they work, but the potency of their healing impacts are clearly evident."*

NLP explores six logical levels for personal transformation, which offer you, the reader, some fun insight into your greatest place of empowerment when it comes to igniting positive change in your behavior and environment along with what you believe is possible in life:

*Spirit => Identity => Beliefs => Capabilities => Behavior => Environment*

Set up in an upside-down pyramid format, with the spirit logical level at the top and the environment level at the bottom, imagine a big funnel flowing down from the top to the bottom, from spirit to environment.

If you create a positive shift in your spirit, your personal relationship with Jesus Christ, then each level below the spirit will experience a positive change. Expanding your spirituality, your relationship with God, in a positive direction is the highest level of personal transformation.

The choice to make a positive shift at the level of your soul creates a domino effect, inspiring and transforming your identity, beliefs, capabilities, behavior, and environment. Every logical level in the pyramid will affect itself and every level underneath it.

As you personally encounter Jesus Christ and invite Him to be the Lord of your life: your mind, will, and emotions begin to experience transformation. When Jesus sits on the throne of your heart, you begin to seek out His wisdom, compassion, and insight in every thought. The former way of "doing you" begins to experience and identify an extreme makeover. And then the fullness of life starts to become your reality: *"I have come that they may have life and have it to the full"* (John 10:10b). *"but be transformed by the renewing of your mind"* (Romans 12:2b).

Your capabilities and beliefs fall between your identity and your behaviors. Your environment is where your behavior happens. Your behavior is what you do, think, and say and is directly influenced by your identity: Who am I? Why am I here? What will it matter?

Many people will come to me as a Master NLP Practitioner, seeking to change their behavior (e.g., stop smoking, get in shape, decrease daily stress, create positive connections at work/home, increase their confidence, release fears/phobias, and stop compulsive behaviors).

I will co-facilitate with the client healthy solutions and explore alternative behavior which shifts the experiences in their day-to-day environment; however, when the client is willing, I will invite them to explore the opportunities to make a change to a higher level, considering that many people's higher-level identity is wrapped up in their behavior.

The behaviors you manifest in your life flow from the highest logical level of your spirit and identity. When you make a shift to a higher level from the highest logical level, your spirituality and your environment will shift accordingly.

Simply put, your soul connection with God drives the rest of your ship in life, how you show up. When you are disconnected from a relationship with God—your highest source of guidance, wisdom, and love—you begin to fragment the rest of your inverted pyramid:

- **YOUR SPIRIT:** Your relationship with God. The side of you as a spiritual creature, and your purpose in life and how it affects your ability to lead. Your relationship with Jesus Christ directly affects the next logical level: your identity.
- **YOUR IDENTITY:** Who you are specifically or rather "whose" you are. Do you know you are chosen by God to be an ambassador for Christ in this world? *"We are therefore Christ's ambassadors, as though God were making his appeal through us. We implore you on Christ's behalf: Be reconciled to God"* (2 Corinthians 5:20).
- Three questions emerge when reflecting on your identity: Who am I? Why am I here? What will it matter? As you anchor your identity in Christ, your confidence, purpose, and inner peace will expand.

- **YOUR BELIEFS:** What you believe and value in life. Do you know what you believe and value? Is it evident to the people entrusted to your care in life? Do you believe that God has plans to prosper you and not to harm you, to give you hope and a future? (Jeremiah 29:11). Do you believe that you can do all things through Christ who gives you strength? (Philippians 4:13). Do you believe that God works all things together for an ultimate good for those who love him and have been called according to His purposes? (Romans 8:28). God adores you and has called you according to His good purposes believing this ignites what you believe you are capable of handling and achieving in this world, which is the next logical level for personal transformation.

- **YOUR CAPABILITIES:** Your gifts and talents, and what you are capable of doing or accomplishing. Think about what help you may need in this area. Are you aware of the specific gifts and talents God has entrusted to your care to make Him recognizable in this world? Perhaps it's a gift for detail and execution? Helping other people? Faith? Teaching? Servant Leadership?

- **YOUR BEHAVIOR:** What you think, say, and do. When you react to something or someone, does it come from a place of self-possession that flows from the flesh or the spirit? Self-confidence controlled by the Holy Spirit results in behavior that is kind, compassionate, humble, gentle, and patient, rather than allowing your emotions be the boss of you, you are the boss of your emotions because the Holy Spirit is guiding your thoughts. Self-confidence controlled by the flesh results in behavior that is self-seeking, demanding, easily offended, insecure, suspicious, manipulative, and never satisfied. Are you sensitive to yourself and those around you?

- **YOUR ENVIRONMENT:** Where what you do actually happens. What sort of environment can you create that reflects your identity in Christ, your beliefs and values, and the capabilities of those you lead, serve, and empower?

When you have a fragmented pyramid, you begin to feel unsafe in certain realms of your life relationships, personal growth, sense of purpose, drive, and motivation.

Two basic human needs are safety and connection. When these starts to slip in your life, your stress hormones begin to have their way with you.

"... *people are slaves to whatever has mastered them*" (2 Peter 2:19). As you reflect on your own relationship with the world, what has mastered you in your life? Is it your environment? Opinions and reactions of other people? The need to be seen, acknowledged, and recognized?

Is it your behavior? My clients who are seeking freedom from compulsive behavior, will often say, "I just can't help myself." This reveals a type of personal enslavement due to allowing some food, substance, situation, or person to master them over time, which in some cases results in a biological addiction.

The stress hormone (cortisol) is linked directly to your emotional state of mind and your heart. Extended emotional stress often leads to personal enslavement, which usually occurs hand in hand with unhealthy outlets. The key to freedom in situations like this lies in your ability to accept where you are, accompanied with a desire for positive personal transformation and a choice to take steps in that direction.

As you explore and expand your connection and relationship with Jesus Christ, the chains that hold you back from personal excellence and empowerment will begin to lose their grip on you.

As you resurrect your remembrance of the divine power that courses through your being, an exhilarating experience of liberation begins to emerge, along with peace and wisdom that passes all human understanding. With increased frequency, you will begin to experience moments that are free from your need to own, control, possess, analyze, and conclude, along with your need to know why things happen as they do and how things will turn out. You will begin to gravitate towards the experience of being in God's presence and understanding His purposes for you on your journey of life.

Being here now in the presence of the One who calls you by name and affirms your worth and value each moment of every day will begin to take on a lighthearted playfulness towards the moment of life in front of your face.

As you draw near to God at the beginning of each day and throughout your day, your authentic God-given nature begins to emerge on the front lines of your life. You are reminded of your expanding value, worth, and purpose. You will no longer rise and fall depending on how the world judges you. The stress you have experienced resulting from endless comparisons, jealousies, and moments of envy will no longer enslave you. Once again, you will gain inner freedom to be you, as you remember yourself as loved unconditionally by God. *"It is for freedom that Christ has set us free. Stand firm, then, and do not let yourself to be burdened again by the yoke of slavery" (Galatians 5:1).*

As I went through divorce and two years of treatment for advanced cancer, back in 2006, two verses from the bible were posted by my bedside. They reminded me that my God-given natural state of being is health and restoration, flowing from my soul into all other aspects of my life, and equipping me with the strength needed to rise above and move through any stressor that unfolds before me:

> *"Do you not know?*
> *Have you not heard?*
> *The Lord is the everlasting God,*
> *    the creator of the ends of the earth.*
> *He will not grow tired or weary,*
> *    and his understanding no one can fathom.*
> *He gives strength to the weary*
> *    and increases the power of the weak.*
> *Even youths grow tired and weary,*
> *    and young men stumble and fall;*
> *but those who hope in the Lord*
> *    will renew their strength.*

They will soar on wings like eagles;
they will run and not grow weary;
they will walk and not faint." (Isaiah 40:28–31).

The next verses reminded me of my main source for wisdom in the midst of my personal challenges through two of life's top stressors at the same time.

*"Who is wise and understanding among you? Let them show it by their good life, by deeds done in the humility that comes from wisdom. But if you harbor bitter envy and selfish ambition in your hearts, do not boast about it or deny the truth. Such 'wisdom' does not come down from heaven but is earthly, unspiritual, demonic. For where you have envy and selfish ambition, there you find disorder and every evil practice.*

*"But the wisdom that comes from heaven is first of all pure; then peace-loving, considerate, submissive, full of mercy and good fruit, impartial, and sincere. Peacemakers who sow in peace reap a harvest of righteousness"* (James 3:13–18).

Step into and explore your own relationship with Jesus Christ on a daily basis—the highest logical level that holds in itself the power to expand and strengthen your identity, beliefs, capabilities, behavior, and environment for your highest good and the good of those around you.

I once heard Mother Teresa speak in person. She said that communion with God is much like a fish in water. This is true. No matter where the fish swims, it is surrounded constantly by the presence of water . . . in, though, and around the fish. When the fish jumps out of the water, it realizes that the water is its life force. When it wiggles its way back into the water, the fish never takes the water for granted again.

## Refresh Your Identity in Christ:

Take time this week to pick out a good read that nourishes your soul and expands your relationship and connection with Jesus.

Carve out 5–20 minutes of your day and sit still, seek, speak, and feel the presence of God within and around you.

You may say, "I never hear the voice of God speaking to me when I ask questions."

When I began to seek out the experience of hearing God's voice in my life, I would sit before him, lay my questions out, and then listen. I heard the silence, which produced an unexpected peace inside my body over time. I then began to respond to my questions the way I thought God would respond. Perhaps I was pulling from years of reading and studying the scriptures and from the writings of history's great spiritual Christian writers to produce answers to my questions. Either way, I believe it opened the portal to my own encounter with the voice of God. I began to say the prayer of Samuel, which is found in the Old Testament (1 Samuel 3:9), when Eli instructed Samuel to pray a simple prayer ("Speak Lord, Your servant is listening") after Eli realized it was God who was speaking to Samuel.

As the days and weeks passed and I continued to show up every day, seeking to hear God speak, I remember thinking, "Why not me?" Then, the voice of God became clearer and more specific to my situations and wonderings. My peace increased as well as my ability to surrender all to God. Having full confidence, like a fish in water, He sustains my life on all logical levels.

The choice to move from your soul into the world creates a place of strength and peace within, which is free from common worldly stressors and threats. When your heart is at peace with the Lord, your body and your life experiences will respond accordingly.

Honor your highest logical level: Your Spirit, your connection with God through Jesus Christ and the power of the Holy Spirit living in and through you. Begin this week by giving yourself the gift of time. Expand awareness of your spiritual connection with God. The world screams and God whispers. Take the time to hear His whisper and record what you hear.

As soon as you wake up begin your day with a prayer of invitation. Give the Lord the first fruits of your day:

*Help me Lord, I know without You in and through me I will forget whose I am which will result in behavior that reflects beliefs that compromise the person I am committed to being in this world. What my identity spills out of me and gets lost in the disease to please and the drug of approval I forget that the strength within me is bigger than circumstance. That strength flows from knowing, You have my back. You are working everything together in my day for an ultimate good. Help me to be quicker today than yesterday to remember whose I am. You are my Lord and my God. I want everything to flow from my relationship with You out into my environment so that when people encounter me today, they walk away feeling loved by You.*

*L.O.V.E. Learning Circle: Clarity of Focus Leads to Accuracy of Response:*

L: **LEARN & LISTEN:** What's in this verse or phrase, tip or technique that will help me anchor my identity in Christ more today than yesterday?

_____

_____

_____

_____

O: **OBSERVE:** My 1–3 gold nuggets I want to remember and pull into behavior:

_____

_____

_____

V: **VISUALIZE:** Visualize integrating the meaningful verses and messages into your daily life. What will you notice to be different in your thoughts, perceptions and behaviors?

_____

_____

_____

_____

E: **EXPLORE:** Explore one specific forward action step you commit to taking in the coming days to help anchor your identity in Christ. Explore what you will notice to be different personally and professionally as you apply today's learnings.

_____

_____

_____

_____

# GOD CAN
# MOVE MOUNTAINS

*"Trust in the LORD with all your heart*
*and lean not on your own understanding;*
*in all your ways submit to Him,*
*and He will make your paths straight" (Proverbs 3:5–6).*

Just recently my son Jacob, gave me a gift. It was a beautiful shirt with this verse written on it.

I was so excited to receive and wear this shirt proudly. Wearing this shirt is a great reminder to trust in the LORD and to submit all areas of our lives to Him.

As I was wearing this shirt one day, God revealed to me that this had been a life verse I was living as it relates to my son.

My son Jacob struggled with drug addiction and was finally delivered from his addiction this year! Praise God.

2014 was a very hard year for Jacob and my family. Jacob was in the greatest battle of his life and was losing a lot of friends to this horrible disease called addiction.

I proclaimed to be trusting God with all areas of my life including His plan for Jacob, however as I recently looked back through my journals a paper fell out from a Women's Bible Study retreat that I attended that year. I began to glance through my notes and responses to some of the questions they were asking.

The theme of the retreat was contentment. Being content in all circumstances.

This was a huge challenge for me as I was NOT content not knowing my son's whereabouts or if I would ever hear his voice again. Being totally out of control with this situation did not result in contentment for me. I was worried, angry, tired, frustrated, and spinning out of control.

One of the questions they asked during the retreat was, *"What do I believe about God in this circumstance?"* We had to identify a circumstance we were walking through currently and contemplate our belief about God.

I wrote: *God is not big enough for Jacob's situation?*

The following question asked: *"What am I trusting in?"*

I wrote: *"Still trusting in myself, need to trust God completely."*

God moved mountains and performed miracles that only God can do in my life and in Jacob's life. Back in 2014 I was trying to be god in my own strength and have things work out according to my plan.

God's plan was MUCH greater than I could have even imagined. Not only did God deliver Jacob from several addictions, He restored Jacob's relationship with Him. Jacob is now on fire for the Lord, preaching the Good News of our Lord and Savior Jesus Christ.

I sit back in awe most days to see God's mighty hand work in my family. Jacob is now encouraging my mom and dad to go back to church and they now attend church, Sunday school, and Bible study together. An entire family's identity has been refreshed, restored, renewed, and reclaimed through Christ!

It took years of patiently waiting on the Lord to answer the prayers I and others had been praying for Jacob.

I learned that misplaced trust in the Lord is silly, God has performed many miracles and can still perform miracles today. God is the same today as He was yesterday as He will be tomorrow. He created the universe and everything in it and I was doubting His work in Jacob's life.

## Refresh Your Identity in Christ:

Carve out some time and find a quiet spot to meditate on today's verse:

> *"Trust in the LORD with all your heart and lean not on your own understanding;*
>
> *in all your ways submit to him, and he will make your paths straight"* (Proverbs 3:5–6).

In what areas of your life do you think God is not big enough to intervene?

Is it in any of these areas and/or situations?

- My health
- My marriage
- My finances
- My relationships
- My job
- My singleness
- My broken heart
- My grieving

In a journal or on a separate sheet of paper answer these three questions for your life. Think of a specific area or situation that you need to give complete control and trust over to God. What do you need to trust God in and lean not on your own understanding in this current situation today?

- What do I believe about God in this circumstance?
- What do I believe about myself as it relates to my current circumstance?
- What am I trusting in?

*Dear God,*

*Please forgive me for not fully trusting You in all areas of my life. When doubt creeps in let me tackle it by proclaiming your word. Please help me to not lean on my own understanding which is limited. I see in part; however, You see in whole. Let me turn over every difficult circumstance to You. When I do, I know that You will make my path straight. It didn't say You would remove these circumstances from my life; however, Your words say that my path shall be straight with You. This is comforting as a straight path is easier to navigate than a path that is spun out of control.*

*L.O.V.E. Learning Circle: Clarity of Focus Leads to Accuracy of Response:*

L: **LEARN & LISTEN:** What's in this verse or phrase, tip or technique that will help me anchor my identity in Christ more today than yesterday?

_____

_____

_____

_____

O: **OBSERVE:** My 1–3 gold nuggets I want to remember and pull into behavior:

_____

_____

_____

_____

V: **VISUALIZE:** Visualize integrating the meaningful verses and messages into your daily life. What will you notice to be different in your thoughts, perceptions and behaviors?

_____

_____

_____

_____

E: **EXPLORE:** Explore one specific forward action step you commit to taking in the coming days to help anchor your identity in Christ. Explore what you will notice to be different personally and professionally as you apply today's learnings.

_____

_____

_____

_____

# HOLDING PATTERN

*"He must become greater, but I must become less"* (John 3:30).

In life, there are times that we will experience holding patterns. What we do during the times of holding patterns is what matters most. Our behaviors during these times can draw us closer to God or push us away from God. The choice is ours.

Webster defines a holding pattern as a course flown by an aircraft while waiting for permission to land; a state of waiting or suspended activity or progress.

I was flying to Atlanta the other week and I was beyond excited when the pilot announced that we were making great time and we would arrive 45 minutes early into Atlanta.

In my fast-paced world, anytime I can get somewhere quicker/faster/sooner it is always a win for me; at least that is what I think in the moment.

Thirty minutes later the pilot announced that there were severe tornado warnings in the Atlanta area, and it was unsafe for us to land. We then proceeded to fly in a holding pattern for over an hour. Like many of the other passengers, I was feeling agitated.

I've noticed that most often in life when we experience a holding pattern, the natural reaction is one of frustration. The frustration stems from a need to wait. Waiting for something requires patience and timing. Trusting in the Lord that His plan is better at that moment than our plan. He must increase so we can decrease to our own timing, pace and agenda.

I had to switch my thought pattern and view holding patterns in a different light. A holding pattern serves a greater purpose. The holding pattern protects your safety until the right conditions unfold allowing you to safely get to your destination.

In our fast-past world, we often believe that faster is better. The pause that is experienced in the disruption of a holding pattern is often needed instead of pushing for something to happen in the wrong timing forcing you into the storm.

I have learned that during these times of uncertainty or suspended activity God is inviting me to refresh my identity in Christ. The verse today has transformed my life during times of holding patterns. I must decrease so that God can increase.

I might think I know what is best, safe, needed for my life at that moment, however, God ultimately knows what is best, safe, needed for me at that exact time. His ways are not our ways. We see in part and God sees in whole.

When I think of holding patterns, I think of Mary, the mother of Jesus. Can you imagine the wait and holding pattern she was in from the time of her immaculate conception to the time of Jesus' death on the cross?

Mary's entire life was wrapped up in one big holding pattern, waiting to see the destination, plan, and purpose unfold for her life and for Jesus' life. This holding pattern changed mankind and our eternal future.

Mary walked in the mess and never took her eyes off the one true God, her Lord and Savior. She trusted that in the holding pattern is where God needed her to be to work through her for a greater good. Mary saw in part; however, God saw in whole. She trusted God to do what was best, safe, and needed not only for her but for all!

During these times of holding patterns we only see part of the story. Just recently, I heard a pastor share a beautiful illustration of how we only see in part.

As a young child this pastor described how he would look up and see the bottom portion off what his grandmother was cross-stitching. If you have ever seen a cross-stitch from the back it can look messy, ugly, and unrecognizable. However, the grandmother looking down on the top of the cross-stitch could see exactly how the cross-stitch was unfolding into a magnificent art form. She saw every detail of this beautiful creation that was unfolding, stitch by stitch in her timing. She was looking top-down, the grandson was looking bottom-up.

At times during the holding pattern, most often we are looking bottom-up and cannot see anything good in our wait. Our view looking up sees life as messy, ugly, and unrecognizable. During these times we can lose our grip on our true identity because we become caught up in the mess.

Holding patterns in life can look like:
- Fertility issues
- Marriage issues
- Family crisis
- Children's issues
- Job issues
- Decisions to be made
- Singleness
- Health crisis
- And many more

The beautiful thing that the Lord is calling us to do during this time is to spend time with Him and ask Him to increase our awareness of His presence and care in this time of waiting so that we can decrease our worry, fear, frustration, and agitation.

During the holding patterns of life, how will you show up, even if it is not the way you planned? I think of the Mercy Me song, *Even If*. Explore the song lyrics below:

*Even If,* by Mercy Me

*I know You're able and I know You can*
*Save through the fire with Your mighty hand*
*But even if You don't*
*My hope is You alone*

*They say it only takes a little faith*
*To move a mountain*
*Well, good thing*
*A little faith is all I have right now*
*But God, when You choose*
*To leave mountains unmovable*
*Give me the strength to be able to sing*
*It is well with my soul*

My prayer is that even in the holding patterns of life, I can utter the words to God even though I might not understand, "*It is well with my soul*".

## Refresh Your Identity in Christ:

Take stock of where you are today. Do you have an area of your life which has left you in a holding pattern? Perhaps it is in your finances, health, relationships, marriage, or your job.

This is a great opportunity to practice patience and wait on the Lord.

> *"Come to me, all you who are weary and burdened, and I will*
> *give you rest"* (Matthew 11:28).

Matthew 11:28 is a great verse to memorize and practice. God wants us to come to Him for refreshment. He is The One that can give you rest during the midst of the storm throughout the holding pattern.

Just like an airplane in a holding pattern takes extra fuel, the waiting times of life provide extra time with God.

God wants to be the pilot of your life during times of stormy holding patterns. Will you let Him increase to the position of senior pilot (Captain) of your life? Is God the co-pilot? Is God even on your plane during the hard times?

Remember, God is the same today as he was yesterday, and as He will be tomorrow. He doesn't move or leave us. We move and God remains (John 15). Are you willing to decrease so God can increase and become the one true pilot in your life as He restores your identity in Him?

Will you be able to say it is well with my soul regardless of the outcome?

As I go to God's Word and count my blessings, as I entrust my heart to His keeping, I am renewed. The season and circumstances may not have changed but my outlook can change as I look for the One who loves me in this interlude.

In what area of your life are you experiencing a holding pattern?

_____

_____

_____

_____

_____

_____

_____

Is your approach causing you frustration?

_____

_____

_____

_____

_____

What shift could you make to alleviate your stress while you wait?

_____

_____

_____

_____

_____

_____

_____

*Dear God,*
*Thank You for remaining the same today as You were yesterday as You will be tomorrow. Please remind me that when I am in the midst of a holding pattern to draw closer to You and Your word. Your word is based in truth and is sharper than a sword and will convict me when I am trying to be the one who is in control. I give the keys of the plan over to You to be the pilot of my life in all circumstances not just some of the circumstances. During my times of wait help me to not get spun out of control and redirect me back to You and Your word. Please help me to "Seek first Your kingdom and righteousness and all these other things will be given unto You." I thank You for knowing what is best for me. I know that I don't always have full understanding and only see in part. Help me to trust You as You see my life in whole and know what is best. Thank You for loving a sinner like me. I am so undeserving of Your love and grace and yet, as I was still a sinner, You sent Your son Jesus to die on the cross for my sins. It is well with my soul. Thank You, dear Father, Amen.*

*L.O.V.E. Learning Circle: Clarity of Focus Leads to Accuracy of Response:*

L: **LEARN & LISTEN:** What's in this verse or phrase, tip or technique that will help me anchor my identity in Christ more today than yesterday?

_____

_____

_____

_____

O: **OBSERVE:** My 1–3 gold nuggets I want to remember and pull into behavior:

_____

_____

_____

_____

V: **VISUALIZE:** Visualize integrating the meaningful verses and messages into your daily life. What will you notice to be different in your thoughts, perceptions and behaviors?

_____

_____

_____

_____

E: **EXPLORE:** Explore a one specific forward action step you commit to taking in the coming days to help anchor your identity in Christ. Explore what you will notice to be different personally and professionally as you apply today's learnings.

_____

_____

_____

_____

# TWO IDENTITY THIEVES: YOUR TO-DO LIST & THE DRUG OF APPROVAL

*"We are therefore Christ's ambassadors, as though God were making his appeal through us"* (2 Corinthians 5:20).

*I*f I am what I do, when I don't, I'm not.

Perhaps you need to pause and re-read the above phrase again . . . take your time now and let it sink in to land where it's meant to be.

I wrote down this phrase at a Wayne Dyer seminar: *If I am what I do, when I don't, I'm not,* that I was invited to attend when I was going through advanced cancer and divorce on changing your thoughts.

That one phrase had a positive impact on my connection to what I do in this world: *If I am what I do . . . when I don't "do", I'm not.* Basically, if my identity has spilled into what I do in life, when I stop doing what I am doing then my sense of identity is lost along with my value.

Wayne also said, *there is no stress in this world, only people thinking stressful thoughts.* Another thought-provoking phrase to ponder in the Lord.

How much of your identity, your sense of worth and value, is directly linked to your ability to check off items on your "to-do" list?

How much of your identity and sense of worth and value is attached to what people think about what you do? The drug of approval?

In this last entry we will explore two identity thieves that have the ability to rob your identity and sense of value right from underneath you in 125 thousandths of a second , (0.125 second), which is how quickly your body's stress response kicks in when you feel threatened (not enough, valued, worthy):

- Your To-do List
- The Drug of Approval

There is nothing wrong with making a To-Do list of the things you want to accomplish in your day. However, your To-Do list will start to rob you of inner peace and confidence when you attach your sense of worth and value to it.

For example, I have a project that I am working on and it will take about six weeks to complete.

In the midst of this project I have my values that are always running under the radar: my relationship with God and family, along with health and wellness.

If my behavior does not make time for personal refreshment, family time as well as daily time in prayer and scripture reading then anxiety begins to increase in my body.

Why? Because I am putting what I do, can or think I should accomplish before what I value most.

When what I check off my To-Do list takes precedence over what I value most in life and my choice of time and attention reflects my attachment to my To-Do list then my sense of identity becomes hitched to something outside of me, rendering me vulnerable to rising and falling emotionally depending upon what I get done . . . or don't get done.

I am left spinning in a vicious prison of doing and feeling good about myself because of what I have done rather than feeling good about myself because of "whose" I am along with my main calling to be Christ's ambassador in this world for God to make His appeal through.

Let's shift into what happens when you attach your identity to what people think about what you do: The Drug of Approval.

> "Whenever you cling to anything in this life—whether it is a certain response from the world; a relationship; a material item or desired outcome—happiness dies and anxiety increases"
> —Anthony de Mello

Since you were little you began to learn very quickly what to do and say to get a desired outcome or response, and your addiction to the drug of approval began. It is similar to a spoiled child, the more you give it, the more it wants.

This addiction of approval is fed by your desire to be acknowledged, approved of, popular, validated and praised. It is as if you are saying, "Please tell me that I am good enough, appreciated, smart enough, and worthy to be loved and accepted."

It is a serpent of a drug and will sap you of any remembrance that you already have everything you truly need within your soul for happiness to occur; along with inner peace and joy: *"I have come that they may have life, and have it to the full"* (John 10:10).

It makes a mockery out of you with the antics you play in life all for a momentary high of being approved of or acknowledged. *Look at me, look at me, look at what I did, accomplished, achieved.*

This innate desire for significance is woven into our human nature and if it is fulfilled by anything other than a personal relationship with God then we will experience the ramifications of emptiness and emotional turmoil. This situation is beautifully illustrated in Luke 24:1–5, notice the words of the two angels to the women:

> "On the first day of the week, very early in the morning, the women took the spices they had prepared and went to the tomb. They found the stone rolled away from the tomb, but

*when they entered, they did not find the body of the Lord Jesus. While they were wondering about this, suddenly two men in clothes that gleamed like lightning stood beside them. In their fright the women bowed down with their faces to the ground, but the men said to them, 'Why do you look for the living among the dead?'"*

Why are you looking for the living: true life, inner peace and confidence, freedom, and joy among the dead? The dead being the shiny objects of the world (accolades, popularity, approval) that can never fully satisfy your hunger to know you are loved and that you matter, not because of what you do, but because of who you are in Christ? God adores you and sees you through the loving, sacrificial atonement of Jesus Christ, period.

You have been saved through faith in Jesus Christ, this is your identity, which does not shift like sinking sand or rise and fall depending upon how others judge you.

Once you experience the indwelling power of Christ within you through the Holy Spirit, what you do in this world is fueled by your love for Christ. You want to make Him recognizable in your words, thoughts, deeds, and actions.

Your To-Do list is fueled with enthusiasm "en Theos" (in God), your relationship and connection to the King of Kings and Lord of Lords . . . all things become possible for you, including your ability to release attachment to what you do.

Go for it 100%, whatever "it" is, God is calling you to do it and have only one attachment, your heart to Jesus' heart and make God recognizable in the world.

Being a visionary and motivated human being is of considerable value. It is when you look to those around you to tell you that you can or cannot do something in life, or you only believe in yourself because someone told you how great you are, that you become vulnerable to the experience of forgetting who you are in Christ along with your connection with your God given inner strengths and abilities.

It is a wonderful practice in life to maintain inner calm and connection in the presence of praise or criticism. In this experience, you are able to remain in *your castle* (connected to God). Remember as with any addiction in life, the more you feed it, the more it consumes you along with your ability to remember who you truly are.

## Refresh Your Identity in Christ:

1. **When you Attach your identity to what you do, your To-Do List**

   Check out this little practice to help add value and purpose to what you do each day:

   Write a "to BE List" below your "To Do List" reminding you of who you want Be in the midst of your Doing. For example, I recently wrote the following To-Be list below my To-Do list:

   - To BE Confident that with God ALL things are possible for me today.
   - To BE filled with love, compassion, and kindness so that what I do with my hands is infused with the love of Christ.
   - To Be authentic, transparent, humble, and surrendered to God's will over my will, releasing attachment to outcomes.

   Take time each day and write your To-Be list below your To-Do list. Your To-Be list reveals the person you want to BE while you DO what you feel God calls you to do and reflects to the world the godly character you wish to reveal through the work of your hands and heart.

2. **When You attach your identity to what people think about what you do. The Drug of Approval:**

   What if we were to release all of the "free rent" we give to anxieties around our desire to be liked, recognized, and approved of? I would imagine we would have a lot of freed up head space to focus on fully occupying the space we are called to occupy with our unique personality signature gifts and talents.

As I went through advanced cancer and divorce at the same time I remember reflecting upon how much energy I wasted worrying about how people responded or didn't respond to what I created or accomplished in life.

I now have a little saying I use when I am emotionally spun and stressed out about anything, circumstance, or human interaction which uncorks instant perspective which I gained walking through the cancer journey:

> *Lauren, can you take this with you beyond the "pine box"? If not delete, identify and adjust your focus on what you value most in this life and choose a response that aligns with the person you are committed to being in this day of life you have been blessed to experience.*

Stress is simply the POWER we give to outside circumstance to define our worth, value and capability.

Elicit the state of behavior you desire to experience.

Remember this: you are here on earth to make God recognizable in the world. You are not here to be liked, you are here to grow in your ability to love, you are Christ's ambassador and God is making his appeal through you.

It's not about what you do, it's about who you are in Christ while you do what you do. Are you Loving? Joyful? Peaceful? Patient? Kind? Gentle? Self-controlled? Faith filled? These are the attributes contained in your natural God given state of being.

Remember whose you are, a child of the living God, and why you have been blessed with another gift of life this day: to give glory to God in your words, thoughts, deeds and actions.

Your identity is in Christ, why are you looking for the living among the dead? Resurrect your worth and value in the One who died to win you over to eternal life.

*Dear Lord,*

*Forgive me for looking for the living among the dead. For seeking the approval from the world around me over Your love and sacrifice. Forgive me for the times I give more authority to what others think about what I do in life than to my authentic value, meaning, significance and worth that can only be found in You. Too often my To-Do list defines my feelings around being enough in this life. Forgive me for forgetting that true life, freedom, and confidence can only be found in the experience of being cherished, forgiven, and loved by You. Come into my heart, mind, will, and emotions. I invite You to sit on the throne of my identity and remind my mind, body, and soul that I belong to You, that You love and adore me and that in You I lack nothing for lasting joy, peace, and life. Have Your way with me in spite of myself. Help me to be quicker today than yesterday in my ability to hear and respond to Your voice behind me saying: This is the Way . . . walk in it.*

*L.O.V.E. Learning Circle: Clarity of Focus Leads to Accuracy of Response:*

L: **Learn & Listen:** What's in this verse or phrase, tip or technique that will help me anchor my identity in Christ more today than yesterday?

_____

_____

_____

_____

O: **OBSERVE:** My 1–3 gold nuggets I want to remember and pull into behavior:

_____

_____

_____

_____

V: **VISUALIZE:** Visualize integrating the meaningful verses and messages into your daily life. What will you notice to be different in your thoughts, perceptions and behaviors?

_____

_____

_____

_____

E: **EXPLORE:** Explore a one specific forward action step you commit to taking in the coming days to help anchor your identity in Christ. Explore what you will notice to be different personally and professionally as you apply today's learnings.

_____

_____

_____

_____

# CONCLUSION & SUPPORT MATERIALS

Congratulations, you have completed the journey of exploring 25 Solutions to Refresh your identity in Christ STOP *Letting the World Be the Boss of You*. Refresh means to give new strength to and invigorate.

The common theme of refreshment and hitting the refresh button in our lives to restore our identity in Christ is exciting. As we wrote this book, the word Abide became apparent as it relates to our identity in Christ.

When we abide in Christ, our identity is certain. When we don't abide, we experience frustration and disappointment. It's like a built-in alarm system that goes off inside us when we start to spill out of ourselves rather than abiding in Christ.

Lean into the visual Jesus offers in John 15 when he talks about the Vine and the Branch . . . apart from Christ we can't produce good fruit. The remedy? Refresh your ability to remain in Christ more today than yesterday. Use transitions as mini-retreats to refresh your mind with Scripture and Prayer or simply being present as the priest Eli encouraged Samuel to say: Speak Lord, your servant is listening, and the Lord spoke to Samuel. (1 Samuel 3)

Ask, Seek, and Knock: *Dear Lord, increase my desire to spend time with you more today than yesterday so that I know who I am in YOU.*

The word abide means to have a life-giving connection to Jesus. Sometimes that connection is broken and needs to be refreshed.

It is our intention that within the lessons contained within this book to make the complex simple, applicable, transferable, and sustainable.

Review your key "take-aways" that you recorded in the L.O.V.E. Learning section at the end of each entry. Use these as actionable steps to implement daily to refresh and refocus your identity in Christ. Strengthen the link to the one and only true creator God through His son Jesus Christ.

Check out a few additional thoughts for you to ponder and verses to read for further refreshment below as you encounter the One who makes ALL THINGS New and invites you into refreshment that flows from experiencing the Freedom that Jesus died to offer all who put their trust in Him:

- Jesus was faithful in all of the ways that the Israelites' were unfaithful as they wandered through the desert towards the Promised Land . . . a journey that should have taken nine days, took 40 years because of disobedience.
- Jesus rebuked the devil in Luke 4:1-10, with Holy Scripture from Deuteronomy that spoke of God's desire for His people to have victory over desire, power, and position (*EdgeGodIn.com, Podcast: How to Rebuke the Devil*).
- Jesus is the New Adam. The tree that contained fruit was restricted from Adam and Eve as a result of their *disobedience* and guarded by an Angel, the result of their disobedience was death (restricted years of life on earth) along with exile from the Garden of Eden. Because of Jesus' *obedience* as the last Sacrificial lamb needed for the ultimate atonement for sin . . . beautifully depicted on the cross when Jesus proclaimed: *It is Finished, which is* the last phrase declared with the drinking of the final cup at the Passover meal. Jesus experienced death on a cross, a cross made from a tree that has NOW become the tree of LIFE to all who believe in His death and resurrection.
- "I am the true vine, and my Father is the vinedresser. Every branch in Me that does not bear fruit He takes away, and every branch that does bear fruit He prunes, that it may bear more fruit. Already you are clean because of the word that I have spoken to you. Abide in me, and I in you. As the branch cannot bear fruit by itself, unless

it abides in the vine, neither can you, unless you abide in Me" (John 15: 1–4).

- Believing is an attachment to, a coming to Jesus, and a receiving from Jesus. It is trusting in Jesus, remaining in fellowship with Jesus, connecting to Jesus so that all that God is for us in Him is flowing like a life-giving sap into our lives. Abiding is believing, trusting, savoring, resting, receiving, and reconnecting.

## Support Scriptures for Further Reflection

- Ask the Holy Spirit: What do you want me to remember from these scriptures? What behavior do I want to practice that reflects my desire to live out what I am learning?
- *Refresh my identity in You Lord, I can't give out what I have not experienced within. Refresh me so that I can be refreshment for all those You have entrusted to my care and bring glory and honor to Your name.*

### Psalm 91

1 *Whoever dwells in the shelter of the Most High*
  *will rest in the shadow of the Almighty.*
2 *They say of the Lord, "He is my refuge and my fortress,*
  *my God, in whom I trust."*
3 *Surely he will save you*
  *from the fowler's snare*
  *and from the deadly pestilence.*
4 *He will cover you with his feathers,*
  *and under his wings you will find refuge;*
  *his faithfulness is your shield and rampart.*
5 *You will not fear the terror of night,*
  *nor the arrow that flies by day,*
6 *nor the pestilence that stalks in darkness,*
  *nor the plague that destroys at midday.*
7 *A thousand may fall at your side,*
  *ten thousand at your right hand,*
  *but it will not come near you.*

8 *You will only observe with your eyes*
    *and see the punishment of the wicked.*
9 *If you say, "The Lord is my refuge,"[b]*
    *and you make the Most High your dwelling,*
10 *no harm will overtake you,*
    *no disaster will come near your tent.*
11 *For he will command his angels concerning you*
    *to guard you in all your ways;.*
12 *they will lift you up in their hands,*
    *so that you will not strike your foot against a stone.*
13 *You will tread on the lion and the cobra;*
    *you will trample the great lion and the serpent.*
14 *"Because they love me," says the Lord, "I will rescue them;*
    *I will protect them, for they acknowledge my name.*
15 *They will call on me, and I will answer them;*
    *I will be with them in trouble,;*
    *I will deliver them and honor them.*
16 *With long life I will satisfy them*
    *and show them my salvation."*

**Additional Refreshment Verses:**

**Proverbs 25:13**

Like a snow-cooled drink at harvest time is a trustworthy messenger to the one who sent him; he refreshes the spirit of his master.

**Proverbs 25:25**

Like cold water to a weary soul it is good news from a distant land.

**Genesis 18:5**

"Let me get you something to eat, so you can be refreshed and then go on your way—now that you have come to your servant."

"Very well," they answered, "do as you say."

**1 Samuel 16:23**

Whenever the spirit from God came on Saul, David would take up his lyre and play. Then relief would come to Saul; he would feel better, and the evil spirit would leave him.

## 2 Samuel 16:14

The king and all the people with him arrived at their destination exhausted. And there he refreshed himself.

## 1 Kings 13:7

The king said to the man of God, "Come home with me for a meal, and I will give you a gift."

## Romans 15:32

so that by God's will I may come to you with joy and together with you be refreshed.

## 2 Corinthians 7:13

By all this we are encouraged. In addition to our own encouragement, we were especially delighted to see how happy Titus was, because his spirit has been refreshed by all of you.

## 2 Timothy 1:16

May the Lord show mercy to the household of Onesiphorus, because he often refreshed me and was not ashamed of my chains.

## Philemon 1:7

Your love has given me great joy and encouragement, because you, brother, have refreshed the hearts of the Lord's people.

## Philemon 1:20

I do wish, brother, that I may have some benefit from you in the Lord; refresh my heart in Christ.

## 1 Corinthians 16:18

For they refreshed my spirit and yours also. Such men deserve recognition.

# ABOUT THE AUTHORS

### JENN CHLOUPEK, M.ED, CSC

Jenn Chloupek is a world-renowned Master Sherpa Executive Coach, facilitator, and trainer. She is the co-author of the *"Why It Matters"* book which is also a concept that is taught internationally both in the public and private sector. Chloupek has over 25 years of experience as an educator, strategic planner, and leader. Jenn has worked with many Federal Agencies as well as numerous Fortune 500 companies. She is currently the Chief Learning Officer at Sherpa Coaching. Her mission is to connect people to their true identity, to tools and resources and to other people in order to champion human potential in Christ. She lives in Scottsdale, Arizona with her husband Lar Chloupek. She loves to travel back to the East Coast to spend time with her two boys Jacob and Colton and with her Mom and Dad.

### LAUREN E. MILLER, M.ED, CSC, PCC

Lauren E. Miller, is a Sherpa Executive Coach, ICF-PCC (International Coach Federation) certified, Master NLP and EFT Practitioner and holds a 2nd Degree Black Belt from the World TaeKwonDo Federation. She holds a Masters in Adult Education with a Certification in Human Resources Development. Through God's mercy, grace, and strength, she has personally conquered two of life's top stressors at the same time, advanced cancer and divorce. Lauren is an SME in stress management, coaching youth and adults. Award Winning Author, Motivational Speaker and HRD trainer, Lauren facilitates fun process driven programs with structure, guidance, support. and accountability designed to create positive change in behavior resulting in a positive impact in one's personal and professional life. She is happily remarried and gratefully enjoys her life in Colorado with her loving husband, three grown children and her first grandchild. Lauren has been active in youth and adult ministries for over 30 years. You will often find Lauren kitchen dancing to her favorite praise and worship music or rolling around on the floor with her two dogs during her free time.

**Lauren's Mission Statement:** To Champion Human Potential in Christ: *Equip people and teams globally with mindset skills and sustainable behavioral shifts to de-stress their lives, regain inner clarity of purpose, and step into personal and professional excellence.*

Explore More at: http://LaurenEMiller.com Click on the store tab in the upper right-hand corner to gain access to support materials for learning and growth.

Listen into the Edge God Podcast at: http://EdgeGodIn.com. Edge God In ministries is dedicated to Championing Human Potential in Christ via online Bible Study Lessons, Educational Seminars and Trainings.

# ADDITIONAL SUPPORT RESOURCES

- Audio Personal Excellence and Wellness CDs including the Stress Solutions for the Soul CD series: Go To: Store Tab at LaurenEMiller.com
- 30 Day, 3 Minute a Day Excellence & Wellness Programs
- Audio/Visual 3 Minute Daily Messages: Use the code: LOVELIFE for a 50% Discount and Go To: https://app.avanoo.com/spa/corp/#/landing/494
- Sign-Up for the free weekly Stress Relief Tip from Lauren on the home page of LaurenEMiller.com.

**Award Winning Books:** Go To: LaurenEMiller.com/stress-relief-books

- *Hearing His Whisper . . . With Every Storm Jesus Comes Too*
- *99 Things You Want to Know Before Stressing Out!*
- *Stress Solutions for the Soul with Pearls of Hope*
- *5 Minutes to Stress Relief*
- *Release the Stress around Breast Cancer*

Contact us at: info@LaurenEMiller.com

*"It is for FREEDOM that Christ has set us free. Stand firm, then, and do not allow yourself to be burdened by the yoke of slavery"* (Galatians 5:1).

*Stop Letting the World be the Boss of You!*

*Refresh Your Identity in Christ*

Made in the USA
Middletown, DE
26 April 2021

37828272R00111